COLIN RYE

change
management

●●●●● the 5-step action kit

REVISED EDITION

KOGAN
PAGE

For Fiona, Timothy and Emily

First published in 1996
Revised edition published in 2001

Kogan Page Limited
120 Pentonville Road
London N1 9JN

© Colin Rye, 1996, 2001

British Library Cataloguing in Publication Data
A CIP record for this book is available from the British Library.
ISBN 0 7494 3380 9

Typeset by Saxon Graphics Ltd, Derby
Printed and bound in Great Britain by Creative Print & Design (Wales) Ebbw Vale

Contents

Introduction

A ROUTE MAP TO THE CHANGE MANAGEMENT 5-STEP ACTION KIT

This book is designed as a toolkit. It is deliberately structured to allow the reader to dip into individual chapters or sections at will. There is no absolute need to read it cover to cover since each chapter stands in its own right.

This book was written to explore and assist the process of Change Management. However, certain sections can, directly or with only minor interpretation or modification, be applied to other circumstances. Figure 1 below illustrates the range of possible applications and identifies the relevant sections.

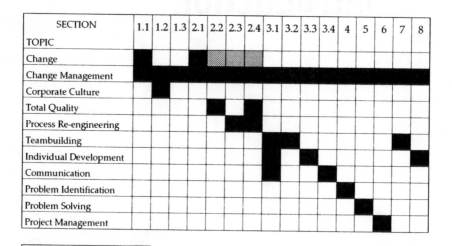

Figure 1

There is also considerable deliberate cross-referencing between chapters and sections, comprehensive referencing to sources of materials included, a full Bibliography and an extensive Index such that readers are directed both within and outside of the Action Kit for further information and reading.

IN SUMMARY ...

The book commences with a discussion of the relationship between change and corporate culture and the implications for Change Management.

THERE THEN FOLLOW:

- Descriptions of Total Quality (TQ) and Business Process Re-engineering (BPR) – two powerful change methods – and a discussion relating to their possible integration.

- An exploration of the issues of Teambuilding, Individual Development and Change Communication and their relationship to the process of change.

- Techniques and models to assist the process of Change Management. These have been drawn together from a wide range of sources and represent my selection from among many. Each is proven insofar as I have personally applied it and benefited from its practical use. My purpose in this book is to share these with other individuals who have, during their daily lives, to invoke or manage the change process. Some of them may be familiar to the reader, some will be new. The selection includes techniques and models commonly used in BPR and during the introduction of TQ. Also included are others which are appropriate to Teambuilding and to Individual Development, both of which are critical to the successful introduction of change but are so often overlooked.

Many of the techniques and models can be employed during more than one stage of a Change Management process. For example, Brainstorming can be used effectively to generate solutions but is equally applicable to many of the issues surrounding then planning and implementation processes. Where this is the case, I introduce the technique or model in the chapter covering the earliest stage to which it is relevant and a reference to later use is included in its description.

For each technique or model I have defined its purpose, the method of operation and my personal observations and comments. I have also noted links to other techniques or models included in the Change Management 5-Step Action Kit and sources of further information. The descriptions are necessarily restricted by the space available. My objective is to whet the appetite of the reader to explore further those that appear most useful.

This revised edition of the book includes, for the first time, a CD ROM, which provides all of the Change Management techniques and models in a convenient form for readers to use in the context of their own Change Management projects. Subject to any third-party copyright restrictions noted, the CD ROM files may be modified as the reader sees fit to meet his specific needs. The files are supplied in Microsoft Office software format and should therefore be accessible to most modern PC systems. The 'CD ROM User Guide' in Appendix 2 (also included as a file in the root directory of the CD ROM) provides full details of the file and document types and, for ease of use, the CD ROM sub-directory structure mirrors the chapters and sub-sections of the book itself.

Change is a fascinating but complex subject – every change situation demands its own unique approach. Change Management is, I believe, an essential skill for every Manager to possess. It is my sincere hope that this book will assist each and every reader in determining the most appropriate approach to any change situation which may arise. If this objective is achieved then the readers will, I hope, find themselves enabled to prove the old adage that change really is as good as a rest!

Part One

The Principles of Change Management

I

Change, Corporate Culture and Change Management

THE NATURE OF CHANGE

What do we know, or believe, about change in the business environment?

It would seem that the characteristics of modern-day change are that:

▌ change is vital if a company is to avoid stagnation;

▌ change is a process and not an event;

▌ change is normal and constant;

▌ the pace of change has increased and is likely to increase further in our fiercely competitive business world and with the speed of technological development;

▌ change can be 'natural', that is, evolutionary or 'adaptive', that is, a reaction to external circumstances and pressures;

▌ change can be 'directive', that is, implemented by 'top-down' management or 'participative', that is, involving those parties impacted by the change;

▌ change can be 'incremental', that is, continuous small changes or 'step', that is, radical shift from current to new processes;

▌ the impact of change is not entirely predictable; change is untidy and planned change often needs adjustment in the light of experience and experimentation;

and perhaps most importantly ...

▌ there is a relationship between change and the organisational environment or culture.

THE INTERFACE BETWEEN CHANGE AND CORPORATE CULTURE

It is apparent that change of whatever form interfaces with three organisational components which effectively constitute the corporate culture, as illustrated in Figure 2 below. Change Management must take account of each of these three components, which are:

- the historical and political evolution of the company;

- the management and organisation of the company;

- the people who work for the company.

Figure 2

History and Politics

The historical and political evolution of a company will have a significant bearing on its acceptance of change. The following questions will be among those to be considered when planning change:

■ Where do the origins of the company lie and what are the associated values? What image does the company like to promote? What perception of the company do customers hold? Are any of these compromised by the proposals for change?

■ What are the origins of individuals within the company? Have they had good or bad previous experiences of change on which their reactions to new change proposals will be based?

■ What are the traditions and norms to which management and employees alike have become accustomed? What long-standing policies and 'rights', both written and unwritten, exist? Are any of these threatened?

■ What is the relationship between the 'powers' within the organisation and those charged with effecting the change? Will these powers 'own' the change?

■ What will be the effect of the change on the 'balance of power' as measured in terms of current owners of resources and expertise? Who will be the 'winners' and 'losers'?

■ Who are the 'winners' and 'losers' in terms of personal status (grade, status symbols and spheres of influence)?

In essence, who are the parties most impacted by the change? Will they resist the change and, if they do, how significant will their influence be on the effective introduction of the change?

Management and Organisation

Change will invariably impact the roles of management and the structure and operation of the organisation. Some of the most likely impacts of modern-day change are:

- senior management take a more strategic stance, encouraging opportunities for progress through innovation and recognising contribution to achievement of business objectives;

- the role of line management shifts from that of 'autocrat' to that of 'facilitator';

- boundaries between jobs, divisions and departments become blurred;

- jobs broaden both in terms of scope and of accountability with the requirement for specialists decreasing and the demand for the multi-skilling increasing;

- project and group work both increase;

- increased harnessing of technology and improving processes reduce the total availability of jobs;

- employees are required to be 'customer-facing' in respect of activities and outputs.

Before embarking upon a significant change it is therefore vital to gauge what proportion of the workforce is able to cope with such shifts and, more importantly, is willing to make the transition required.

People

Although identified against alternative headings, it must be pointed out that every single issue noted above is in fact a 'people' issue. It is impossible to invoke even the most modest of changes without impacting the manner in which someone works. Thus, it is appropriate simply to add a small number of cautionary prompts for those invoking change:

1. Even for the smallest of changes, don't underestimate the reactions of those impacted.

2. Recognise that typically with change there comes an expectation of a reward for acceptance in terms of pay, promotion or other form of recognition.

3. Think through carefully the impact of the change on every job it affects.

Each of the above should be considered alongside the key issue of the manner in which the change will be determined and invoked. Is the process of change to be fully participative, to be consultative or merely to be communicated as a *fait accompli*?

THE IMPLICATIONS FOR CHANGE MANAGEMENT

In order to understand change and therefore to be able to manage it effectively, consider your own reactions to change. You will need to recognise that people's reactions are many and varied and are very dependent upon the manner in which it is proposed that the change is to be effected. Nevertheless, typically, you should expect:

■ **shock** – particularly if significant change has not been the norm for the organisation or individual;

■ **anxiety** – particularly if the consequences of the change are uncertain and likely to remain so for a significant period of time;

■ **anger** – particularly if individuals feel they have no say in the nature of the change and its implementation, as well, perhaps, as disliking its specific implications for them as individuals;

▊   **expectancy** – there are those, frequently in the minority, who
relish the prospect of change and the opportunities it may
bring.

Three out of four of the above can be considered negative reactions
which may result in resistance to proposed change. It is not unrea-
sonable to suggest that a similar ratio of unfavourable to favourable
reactions will be typical of the workforce. Below I explore methods by
which these odds can be improved. This is the substance of Change
Management.

The paragraphs which follow can be regarded as hints and tips for
successful change. Many you will consider to be common sense but
isn't it so often the case that it is failing to do the blindingly obvious
that catches us out?

Within these paragraphs people and communication issues, which I
believe to be the keys to successful change management, have been
highlighted respectively by *italicisation* and underlining. Bracketed,
(**emboldened**) references refer the reader to some of the techniques
and models from within the chapters containing tools and techniques
which can be used to assist the change processes.

Cultural Backdrop

▊   Prepare *people* to expect change in their careers as they expect it in
the stages of their domestic lives.

▊   Cultivate an environment in which continuous improvement is an
expectation of every *employee*.

▊   Educate staff about *people's* typical reactions to change, that is, the
shock, anxiety, anger and expectancy referred to previously **(see
pages 119–20)**.

▊   Establish effective Change Management as part of the normal role
of every line manager and reward high performance in this
respect.

Identifying Opportunities for Change

■ Use *multifunctional groups* to identify opportunities for improvement.

■ <u>Solicit ideas</u> for change and ensure that the best receive some form of recognition but do stress to instigators that not all may be progressed **(see pages 68–73)**.

Planning Change

■ Ensure that the current situation, structures and working methods – the 'platform' for change – are fully understood through <u>consultation</u> with those involved **(see pages 48–64)**.

■ Develop and <u>communicate</u> a vision of the future together with a credible and honest explanation of why change is required. The 'case for action' must be concise, comprehensible and, above all, compelling **(see pages 91–92)**.

■ Determine what needs to occur to move from the current to the future scenario **(see pages 61–62)**.

■ Plan the implementation period carefully by identifying chronologically the likely transitional states and determining the most streamlined paths to the desired future **(see pages 63–64 and 82–84)**.

■ Determine how the change process will be overlaid on day to day activities.

■ Involve the *people* impacted by the change in the planning process such that their commitment is gained and they are motivated to support the change **(see pages 103–04)**.

■ Define and <u>communicate</u> objectives, responsibilities and timescales carefully.

▪ Seek advice on implementation methods and timescales from 'experts' who understand, and/or are responsible, for areas of operation affected.

▪ Meet with others who have successfully implemented change to understand their methods and feedback in respect of your own plans.

'Championing' Change

▪ Gain high level commitment by 'championing' the change with those whose support is critical.

▪ Identify 'change champions', that is, those who relish change and have 'bought-in' to your proposals, and gain their active support and involvement in the <u>promotion</u> of your intentions.

▪ Positively <u>communicate</u> your vision of the situation after the change **(see pages 86–87 and 91–92)**.

▪ <u>Offer evidence</u> of success elsewhere within or outside of the company.

▪ Involve *employees* in celebrating successes, particularly in the early stages of the transition.

▪ Explain how *employees* will be equipped with skills, as necessary, to complete their new jobs.

▪ Identify a small number of key benefits of the change and <u>promote</u> these heavily.

Countering Resistance

▪ <u>Describe</u> the change and its repercussions, both positive and negative, honestly to *those impacted*.

■ <u>Communicate</u> the change, implementation proposals, progress, schedule adjustments, etc promptly – beat the grapevine!

■ Set up specific <u>formal channels of communication</u> for all issues relating to the change, eg notice boards.

■ Expect resistance and develop strategies to overcome it. This may involve gaining the commitment of *individuals* and *groups* such that critical mass favouring the change is achieved.

■ Identify and address the structural and procedural barriers to the change.

■ <u>Advise</u> the *people* of the likely impacts of the change and concentrate on <u>listening</u> to their reactions rather than endeavouring to 'sell' the change.

■ Allow *people* to express their feelings, particularly if they express loss of something presently held dear.

■ Welcome feedback in which *employees* express their views regarding the change and the progress of the change.

■ Ensure that reward systems are adjusted to take account of new measures of performance and new accountabilities.

Implementation

■ Pilot the change wherever possible involving *volunteers* in the process.

■ During the implementation, involve the *people* impacted so that they are motivated to support it.

■ Make yourself available to the *people* impacted for <u>consultation</u> and <u>discussion</u>.

- Share whatever information pertaining to the change that you can.

- Monitor implementation progress against the implementation plan and adjust as necessary.

Post Implementation

A change of any significance should by subject to a Post Implementation Review the objectives of which are:

- objectively, to assess the change against the original objectives and to measure and compare the costs and benefits of the change against the original cost-justification;

- subjectively, to assess the effectiveness of the change itself and the methods of implementation through reference to those involved in the new process. This should be achieved by face to face discussion but may be complemented by attitude surveys and questionnaires so as to include a wider audience.

It is strongly recommended that all results, both favourable and adverse, are shared with the workforce as a whole since positive proof that a need for change was accurately identified and met, or the humility to 'own up' to having made a mistake will generate the respect of the organisation's employees and provide a better platform for future change.

2

Types of
Change

INTRODUCTION

Change comes in many shapes and sizes.

A modification to a procedure represents change as does the introduction of a new computer system and, as previously suggested, it is impossible to invoke even the smallest change without impacting the manner in which someone works.

Consider, for example, the advent of electronic mail. You might assume that e-mail would be welcomed throughout an organisation as a sophisticated new means of improving the speed and quality of communication but let's examine the consequences against the previously suggested interfaces with the corporate culture.

History and Politics

■ If it has been 'politically correct' in the past to address certain members of the organisation only by means of formal memoranda or, indeed, not to be allowed to communicate with those in the higher echelons of the hierarchy at all, what are the repercussions for communications in the brave new world of e-mail?

■ If traditionally senior managers have been entitled to personal secretaries whose role is threatened with extinction or by a shift to becoming mere departmental typists because of an anticipated reduction in typing workload, what is the perceived impact on the status of senior managers?

■ How will senior management react to an expectation that they must type messages themselves?

Management and Organisation

■ If e-mail is to be introduced, who will 'own' the system and take responsibility for its management, operation and maintenance?

Does ownership of such a corporate system shift the balance of power in favour of that individual?

▪ If e-mail access to certain areas or hierarchical levels of the organisation is to be barred, how will this be achieved in practice? Will new procedures also be introduced to advise access levels or will the system itself be programmed to 'police' the flow of communication? Who will have the right to define the parameters?

▪ What are the structural repercussions of the potential displacement or redeployment of secretarial and typing resources?

People

▪ If secretarial or typing resource is displaced or redeployed, what will be the effect on the morale of those individuals and how will this 'contaminate' those working with or around them?

▪ How will the workforce react to the advent of e-mail? Will people relish the opportunities of easy access and of being more easily accessible?

▪ What will be the impact on normal daily working life? Will e-mail recipients become obsessed with dealing with their e-mail 'in-basket' to the detriment of potentially more significant work?

▪ Will e-mail impact interpersonal relationships? Will people cease talking to one another on the telephone or face to face and simply pass messages or will e-mail release them from unwanted interruptions and enable greater focus on the more important tasks?

▪ What about training? How computer-literate is the workforce? How receptive will people be to typing messages previously processed by the corporate typing resource? Will everyone be an e-mail user and, if so, how can mass training best be delivered?

The above serves to illustrate just how complicated the Change Management of a seemingly innocuous change can be. The questions posed merely skim the surface and yet these and many more besides have to be addressed. Typically, the more significant the change – the longer the list!

Two methods which invoke very significant levels of change at the present time are Total Quality (TQ) and Business Process Re-engineering (BPR) and these are the subjects of the following two sections.

TOTAL QUALITY (TQ)

TQ comprises change invoked through four key components – systems, processes, people and management.

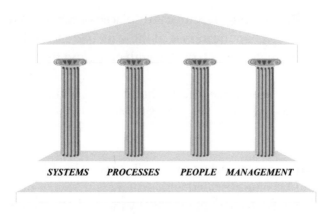

SYSTEMS   PROCESSES   PEOPLE   MANAGEMENT

Figure 3

As illustrated in Figure 3, these can be depicted as the four pillars of TQ. This is entirely appropriate since TQ is deemed to be the supporting structure which underpins the manner in which the organisation operates and everything the organisation does. Furthermore, if each pillar and the roof of the organisational structure are seen to represent 20 per cent of organisational problems, the pillars – 80 per cent of the total – constitute problems which can be addressed by the workforce as a whole while the 20 per cent represented by the roof must be addressed by those operating at the more senior levels of the organisation.

TQ is best defined as 'meeting customer requirements' in a context in which every individual in the organisation is a customer of the process preceding their own, and a supplier to the process succeeding their own. Thus customers are internal to the organisation as well as external (see Figure 4).

Additionally, 'TQ is a competitive concept because it is concerned with being the "best", where "best" is defined by the marketplace rather than by the product or service provider' and the best companies will achieve 'a level of superiority that is unusually high'.[1] Customer focus is the essence of TQ.

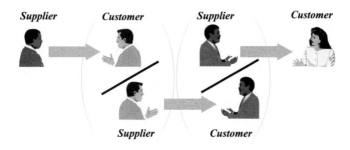

Figure 4

The Four Pillars of Total Quality

TQ is often perceived as being a very 'soft' or informal method of introducing change. In reality, true TQ is a very rational technique which is driven by hard statistical evidence of the need for change and for systems and processes to support both the change and the ensuing operations.

---

[1] Hutchins, D (1992) *Achieve Total Quality*

Systems

The need for change will be identified in a number of ways, most notably:

1. *Statistical Process Control*: this is the accurate and continuous measurement of quality and is typified by the measurement of frequency of failure – how often and where concentrated and the analysis of cause and effect **(see pages 56–57)**.

2. *Benchmarking*: TQ demands the identification of best practice (for each process on an industry and preferably worldwide basis) recognising that best practice is only best until someone else begins to do it better. Thus constant monitoring and awareness of best practice is demanded.

The standards of best practice are set by the organisation's competition as well as by customers demands. However, TQ recognises that customers will perceive a quality degradation from the current supplier as competitors exceed current best practice. TQ further recognises that customer needs are often unnecessarily exceeded with products and services being over-specified and over-engineered at the whim of the producer or supplier. This is regarded as unnecessary perfectionism.

After the change has taken place, the quality of operations will be supported by:

1. *Quality Control (QC)*: while often confused with post-production inspection, QC is, in fact, the generic term for ongoing statistical measurement of quality as defined above. It thus implies the application of preventative controls intended to pre-empt defects and failures by trend monitoring.

2. *Quality Assurance (QA)*: is preventative. QA entails the provision of documented procedures to ensure design, development and

operations result in products and services which meet customer-contracted requirements. The British Quality Standards BS5750 and its European and International counterparts (EN29000 and ISO9000) are QA standards. None of these, however, can be considered as TQ. They constitute a possible component of a quality programme but in the absence of the others described here typically represent mere 'policing'.

3. *Foolproofing*: is a further system for preventing defects and failures. Typically IT-driven, foolproofing uses computer systems to monitor processes. These will, for example, alert machine failures which, whilst not stopping the process, would otherwise result in substandard products.

Processes

TQ regards every activity of an organisation as a part of a process. In so doing, it encourages the constant review of processes in three ways:

1. *Project by Project Improvement*: TQ companies promote and facilitate the concept of continuous, incremental improvement throughout the organisation. Indeed, 'TQ implies the use of a disciplined and structured approach to project by project improvement activities where the goal is to achieve a faster rate of improvement than any competitor or rival'.[1]

2. *Waste Elimination*: the elimination of waste can only be effectively achieved if the volume of waste is known. In TQ companies this will be achieved by statistical process control. This will, for example, measure defective products written-off or customer complaints in a service environment. TQ differentiates between inspection and failure (QC) and prevention (QA). It recognises that 'it does not matter how much you inspect a bad product, it will not

---

[1] Hutchins, D (1992) *Achieve Total Quality*

make it any better; and all inspection does to a good product is to add to its cost'.[1] TQ defines failure in terms of rework, modification, high inventory (because of inefficient production processes), product recalls, customer complaints, etc and promotes the conversion of effort expended on inspection and dealing with failures into time spent on preventative measures **(see pages 66–67)**.

3. *Process Chain Re-engineering*: this concept revolves around the roles of individuals and groups being seen not only as that of customer and supplier but also that of a 'processor' who discusses his own needs with his suppliers and is fully aware of his customers' needs such that those interactions which are critical to high performance can be identified. Once these key process constituents are known, it is possible to address any causes of substandard performance, implement remedial and/or other measures and monitor the impact on the total process chain.

Two possible outcomes of process improvement are:

1. *Just In Time Production (JIT)*: also known as 'stockless production'. JIT is the elimination or minimisation of the stock which is often held as a safeguard against inefficiencies in the overall production process. It typically demands the utilisation of sophisticated systems and procedures to control the flow of parts and schedule the elements of the production cycle. It will also often involve close partnership arrangements with suppliers.

2. *Total Productive Maintenance (TPM)*: relying once more upon statistical control, TPM is achieved through the uninterrupted operation of the production line. It involves the measurement of 'mean time between failure' (mtbf) of those components of the production process which are subject to breakdown or other failure. Accurate measurement of the mtbf enables the

---

[1] Hutchins, D (1992) *Achieve Total Quality*

preventative replacement of such components prior to their anticipated failure thus eliminating the disruption which goes with unscheduled maintenance.

People

TQ companies value their employees both as individuals and for their contribution to the growth of the company. The value placed on the quality of individuals is demonstrated in a number of ways:

Individual Ability and Attitude

- *Recruiting the Best*: where best implies the highest calibre of staff at all levels. TQ companies strive to earn themselves a reputation which will attract the best school-leavers and graduates.

- *Lifelong Learning*: having recruited a high standard of employee, TQ companies will then commend to them the concept of continuous (lifelong) learning. Employees will be encouraged to explore various means of continuing their school or university education in both academic, personal and job-related skill terms. Line management will be expected to coach their subordinates and to act as mentors as required.

- *Elimination of Specialisation*: given that TQ processes slice horizontally through organisational structures, TQ companies do not favour specialisation which tends to create vertical divisions and introduces jargon to the extent that a 'common language' ceases to exist within the organisation. They also believe that specialisation encourages short-termism both on the part of the individual who will tend to seek career opportunities in their own field, and of the employer who, knowing this, is reluctant to invest in employee education and development.

25

– *Attitude Surveys*: represent a further form of statistical measurement and are used within TQ companies to determine and, consequently, address the issues and attitudes of the workforce.

■ **Contribution**

– *Suggestion Schemes*: TQ-company culture is very receptive to employee suggestions for improvement and will reward good ideas.

– *Quality Circles*: TQ advocates the notion that management must address the major problems and strategic issues but that only the workforce as a whole can identify and address the hundreds of minor inefficiencies, problems and opportunities for improvement. It is appreciated that these minor issues probably represent 80 per cent of all problems and that while they may only account for 20 per cent of problem-related costs, there is a tremendous spin-off benefit in terms of employee morale and motivation achieved by facilitating their involvement. Quality Circles, in which small groups debate ideas for improvement and progress their implementation (once approved at a higher level) provide the forum and are often regarded as the powerhouse of TQ.

Management

The TQ environment must be stimulated by the values, attitudes and actions of management at the highest levels within the organisation. Line managers will be expected to believe in and demonstrate commitment to maintaining the TQ culture of empowerment, involvement and continuous improvement.

■ *At Board level, this involves*:

– *Vision and Mission*: setting and communicating, in terms comprehensible throughout the organisation, a vision for the future and a series of stepping stones to that vision towards the achievement of which all may contribute.

- *Critical Success Factors (CSFs)*: the 'Mission Statement' facilitates the establishment of CSFs. These are goals or targets, the achievement of which indicate a step towards the achievement of the overall Vision. These goals or targets provide a framework and direction within which continuous improvement activities can be progressed.

- *Organisation for Quality*: providing through facilitative Steering Groups or a 'Quality Council', a structure which allows Quality Circles to flourish and proposed improvement activities to be implemented in a co-ordinated manner which accords with the previously-defined CSFs.

At all managerial levels, maintenance of TQ and the TQ culture involves:

- *Project Identification*: taking responsibility both for identifying and for facilitating the identification by subordinates of improvement projects and being prepared to 'own' them.

- *'Championing'*: demonstrating commitment to the corporate Vision and actively promoting improvement projects.

- *Empowerment*: devolving power and authority to staff and providing coaching in order that, in due course, they become able to manage their own daily activities.

- *Recognition and Celebration*: recognising and celebrating contribution and success.

BUSINESS PROCESS RE-ENGINEERING (BPR)

In common with TQ, BPR has four key components – business processes, management and measurement, jobs and structures, and values and beliefs. If TQ is perceived as the four pillars of the organisation, then BPR, a much more 'top-down' managed form of change,

27

is probably best represented by the roof supports or cornices (see Figure 5).

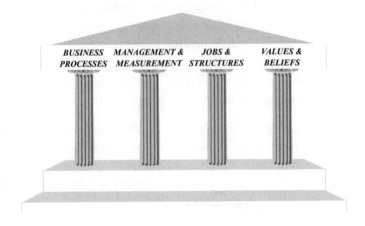

Figure 5

BPR is best defined as 'the fundamental rethinking and radical redesign of business processes to achieve dramatic improvements in critical, contemporary measures of performance'.[1] For clarity, it is appropriate also to define what BPR is not. BPR is not automation, restructuring or reorganisation, or delayering although these may be consequences of a BPR exercise. It is also helpful to consider why a corporation might contemplate BPR given its radical nature. There are three probable reasons:

1. The business is failing and there is no option but to invoke radical change.

2. Business difficulties are foreseen and pre-emptive measured are deemed necessary to avoid business failure.

3. The organisation, rather than 'resting on its laurels', wishes to build on its success and invokes radical change to widen its lead over the competition.

---

[1] Hammer, M and Champy, J (1993) *Re-engineering the Corporation*

There are also a number of significant supporting factors and explanations:

▪ Other initiatives such as streamlining, automation, the resolution of identified existing problems or the continuous minor improvements of a TQ culture have not delivered adequate business advantage.

▪ End-to-end delivery has become too complex and too time consuming with too many people involved (and therefore no-one accountable), too many hand-offs, and too great a need for bureaucratic controls.

▪ 'Classical business structures that specialise work and fragment processes are self-perpetuating because they stifle innovation and creativity in the organisation.'[1] They also demand the presence of excessive layers of managerial hierarchy to draw together fragmented work. These render it unduly difficult to introduce new work practices.

▪ The business world is rapidly changing, highly competitive and customer-driven and current methods are introspective rather than customer facing.

The Four Cornices of Business Process Re-engineering

Business Processes

The essence of BPR lies in the adoption of a 'process orientation'. The characteristics of such an orientation are:

▪ *'Cradle to Grave'*: whether the organisation is concerned with products or services or both, process orientation demands that the delivery process negates organisational boundaries. Thus, as

---

[1] Hammer, M and Champy, J (1993) *Re-engineering the Corporation*

illustrated in Figure 6 for example, the vertical functions of design, manufacture, distribution and sales might be replaced by the single, comprehensive and cross-functional process of 'delivering the product'.

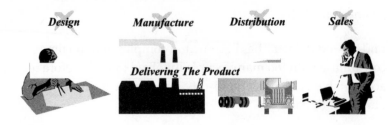

Figure 6

■ **_Multidimensional_**: cross-functional working combines many tasks into one job or process and, in so doing, eliminates hand-offs, reduces administrative overheads associated with controlling the previous fragmented steps and provides a single point of contact for process-related queries.

■ **_Multi-Variant_**: as required, multiple variants of the single process may exist rather than a single standard and potentially unduly complex approach. Variants are tuned to market (customer) needs.

■ **_Multi-User_**: multiple users adopt common processing methods. For example, instead of different divisions or departments procuring stationery by methods of their own invention, each adopts the single corporate process and, with it, the associated economies of scale.

■ **_IT-enabled_**: IT represents a 'solution looking for a problem' in that there is great encouragement of the examination of new technologies and subsequent identification of problems which they might address.

▨ ***Continuous Improvement***: BPR recognises continuous improvement in the form of process maintenance and continual re-examination and redesign of processes which, with time, may once more become fragmented.

Management and Measurement

The achievement of a process orientation demands:

1. ***Process Mapping***: existing processes are process-mapped to establish what currently happens and why, that is, to develop an understanding of the current process **(see pages 58–60)**.

2. ***Prioritisation***: those processes which represent the fundamental core of the business are identified and prioritised for re-engineering based upon which are obviously 'broken', ie exhibit symptoms of failure or gross inefficiency, which are of the greatest importance to customers, and which are the most feasible to re-engineer, ie offer the greatest probability of success.

3. ***Benchmarking***: world-wide cross-industry process comparisons may then be used to establish 'best practice' and provide a possible basis for process redesign.

4. ***'Blue-Sky Thinking'***: the results of benchmarking are integrated with 'blue-sky thinking'. This is the reinvention of the total process and deliberately disregards current practice and norms.

5. ***Process Ownership***: each new process is implemented and a 'Process Owner' is appointed. This individual, who is generally of senior status within the organisation, takes responsibility for the process and its ongoing maintenance.[1]

---

[1] 'Process Owners' may be appointed prior to re-engineering and become the 'change champions'

In the process re-engineered environment there is:

■ **Workforce Empowerment**: employees are empowered within a framework of performance measurement. Process-team working enables members of the workforce to make managerial decisions within the process and the combination of autonomy with measured performance provides accountability.

■ **A Managerial Coaching Role**: the consequence of such managerial empowerment is that management adopt a new leadership role – that of coach. Their concentration will be upon issues of motivation, which is fuelled by the employees' knowledge of performance measures against which they will be assessed and of reward through revised compensation systems.

Jobs and Structures

The results of process re-engineering are typically the following:

■ **Flat Structures**: a process rather than functional orientation which, together with process-teams performing managerial functions, reduces bureaucracy and the requirement for complex, multi-layer managerial hierarchies **(see pages 50–51)**.

■ **Wide Spans of Control**: a less hierarchical structure, workforce empowerment and a managerial role focused on the coaching of subordinates means that managers will have, and can manage, greater numbers of subordinates reporting directly to them **(see pages 50–51)**.

■ **Whole-Process Teams**: traditional departments are replaced by groups of individuals who have the wherewithal to complete a whole process. Typically, this demands greater multi-skilling of individuals and consequently improves job satisfaction.

- *Virtual Teams*: short-term, part-time involvement in multiple teams is also commonplace. Effectively, the individual's time is divided (in respect of areas of work involvement) rather than the component parts of the process.

- *Lateral Career Movement*: flatter structures imply less 'vertical' opportunity for career development. However, individual jobs are of increased dimensions and thus more fulfiling. 'Mastery' necessarily takes longer to achieve and lateral moves are likely as individuals seek to broaden their areas of process-expertise.

- *Job Specification*: job descriptions will be comprehensive and include details of required levels of key competencies such that increased objectivity and accuracy can be applied to selection and appointment processes.

- *Performance Measures*: job descriptions will also detail the performance measures against which jobholders will be appraised.

- *Education*: knowing 'how to' (skills training), while important, is placed alongside 'knowing why' in the process-orientated organisation. The expectation of employees is that they will understand the process in which they are involved and the manner in which the component parts of a process interrelate.

- *Elimination of Checking*: checking and auditing elements of jobs are largely eliminated. BPR, in common with TQ, recognises that the costs of 'policing' can quickly become disproportionate to the cost of producing the product or delivering the service itself. The need for checking and reconciliation is also minimised by reducing the number of hand-off points **(see pages 62–63)**.

Values and Beliefs

Creating and sustaining a process orientation demands:

■ *Living the Values*: senior management lead by example. For example, by demonstrating the notion of being customer-facing by spending appropriate amounts of time with customers providing, and receiving, feedback on service.

■ *Employee Beliefs*: genuine belief throughout the workforce that every individual's job is vital and that teamworking is the only sensible approach to value-adding operation.

■ *Remuneration Expectations*: an explicit, and thus culture-shaping, relationship between customer service and remuneration directly linking the extent to which one maximises the satisfaction of customers to salary and bonuses. Re-engineered companies typically operate flat salary structures since jobs are graded in accordance with competency demands and earnings fluctuations result only from bonuses paid for exceptional performance at managerial discretion.

THE INTEGRATION OF TQ AND BPR

There is a perception that TQ and BPR cannot coexist because they are contradictory methods of invoking change. This is a false and unfortunate perception since the two applied together and with understanding and sympathy offer a tremendously powerful recipe for building, or rebuilding, a corporation. This section explores the fundamental similarities and differences between the two and, in so doing, seeks to demonstrate how they might best be integrated.

Founding Principles

Total Quality	Business Process Re-engineering
Systems	Management and Measurement
Processes	Business Processes
People	Values and Beliefs
Management	Jobs and Structures

Figure 7

As indicated earlier, TQ and BPR each have four identifiable founding principles which are summarised in Figure 7 above. There is a striking similarity between the four pairs of characteristics in that:

- both TQ and BPR value objectivity and derive this, in part, through the use of measurement systems including statistical analysis and benchmarking;

- both promote a process orientation although there is a difference of emphasis. TQ focuses on improvement of customer/supplier relationships (both internal and external) while BPR, wherever possible, consolidates functions to eliminate customer/supplier hand-offs;

- both demand change of people's attitudes and of their values and beliefs. Both promote empowerment and involvement and highly value teamwork whether in Quality Circles or Process Teams. Both underpin the devolution of power with accountability, performance measurement and with reward schemes which recognise exceptional performance;

- both impact the role of management, requiring a coaching and facilitating rather than directive stance. Both introduce the concept of managers as 'Change Champions'. Both impact jobs and structures, reducing the need for management to be power-brokers, authority-giving bureaucrats or a 'police force' which monitors the activities of the workforce minions.

Customer Orientation

TQ and BPR both emphasise the importance of the customer. The expressions 'customer-focus', 'customer-facing', 'putting the customer first' and 'meeting customer needs' litter management texts relating to both.

Approach to Effecting Change

Change through TQ is effected through continuous improvement – incremental change – and is a 'bottom-up' approach to invoking change. This does not imply that top-management instigation and support are not required. It implies that the requirement is to facilitate the creation of Quality Circles and project teams with the authority to investigate working practice and recommend change which top-management will sanction as appropriate. TQ recognises the probability that 80 per cent of problems are best addressed by those closest to, and thus best acquainted with, their causes.

BPR effects change through radical reinvention – step change – and is a 'top-down' approach to change instigation. BPR recognises that 20 per cent of an organisation's problems must be addressed by top-management since it is neither reasonable nor desirable to expect the lower echelons of the corporate hierarchy to be able to identify, let alone solve, major issues of strategy, policy or of organisation. Equally, it would not be either appropriate or acceptable for them to recommend, and therefore be accountable for, change impacting these areas.

Change Formulation

This suggested 80/20 split of corporate problems and issues and its associated demands on those at different levels of the organisation mirror the expectations of TQ and BPR in terms of the thought processes which underlie change proposals. TQ generally demands deductive or analytical thinking. Such thinking stems from measurement, comparison, fact-finding and reasoning, all of which might reasonably be expected from members of a Quality Circle. BPR, on the other hand, demands inductive or conceptual thinking rooted in supposition, intuition, lateral thinking and raw creativity – typically abilities associated with more senior management.

The Role of Information Technology

These modes of thinking parallel the difference in the role of IT. In the TQ environment, IT tends to be used to automate or to foolproof processes. In a BPR context, technological development is closely monitored and the potential of IT is explored in order to find operational problems which newly-available technologies can address and to find opportunities to exploit IT to grow the organisation in both new and existing business areas.

Change Culture

The final significant difference between TQ and BPR is the impact of each on the corporate culture. The well-worn phrase which reflects the attitude change which the advent of TQ demands is 'it's just the way we do things around here'. The cultural shift to which this relates is one which expects of every employee a constant focus on the ultimate customer and a continuous drive for improvement in working practice. BPR is different, most often being a programme of change with an identifiable beginning and end, albeit with an ongoing requirement for process maintenance and review. This does not suggest that there is no impact of BPR on corporate culture. Indeed, it is probably fair to expect greater resistance to change from such an 'initiative' or 'project' than to changes emanating on a regular basis from a TQ culture which has permeated organisational thinking.

Integration

It should by now be clear that TQ and BPR share some common ground but are essentially entirely different means of invoking change. To believe that they are compatible one has first to 'buy-in' to the suggested split of organisational problems and issues. Whether 80 per cent/20 per cent or any other variation, it is apparent that TQ is ideally suited to addressing the bottom end of the range and BPR to the top. It should also be pointed out that a major BPR exercise, while addressing major strategic issues, will almost invariably create a whole host of minor operational ones which TQ can address. Thus not only is integration possible, it is probably highly desirable.

3
Teambuilding, Individual Development, Change Communication

In previous chapters we have established that on the interface between Change Management and corporate culture lie issues of people and of communication. We have also suggested that, to a greater or lesser extent, resistance to change is inevitable. When introducing change, the goal must therefore be to minimise the level of resistance. This chapter explores how this may be achieved through a combination of enabling those affected by the change to be involved in its design and implementation and through appropriate and effective communication of change.

GAINING COMMITMENT

Figure 8 seeks to illustrate how appropriate development of people, both as individuals and as members of teams, and effective communication can lead to the required commitment to change – commitment being the final ingredient in the recipe for successful change management.

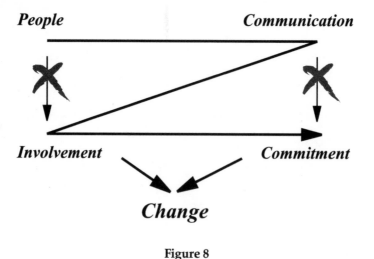

Figure 8

This model deliberately identifies what some might regard as shortcuts in gaining commitment. There are no shortcuts! It is unrealistic to expect commitment to be generated by a level of involvement which is not underpinned by a detailed understanding of the context of the change acquired through effective communication. It is equally unrealistic to expect commitment to be generated by effective communication but in an environment which denies people the opportunity to get involved.

Anything less than genuine commitment will not generate real ownership of the change and will fail in the medium to long term.

TEAMBUILDING

Involvement implies being or becoming part of the team effecting, and operating in the aftermath of, change. Chapter 7 provides a substantial number of techniques and models for teambuilding purposes. These are neither complicated nor sophisticated but rather a selection of simple tools to aid interpersonal understanding and promote cohesive action. It should be pointed out that some of the techniques included relate to facets of the individual which manifest themselves in a team setting.

INDIVIDUAL DEVELOPMENT

At the truly individual level, invoking, understanding and managing change may demand personal development and the acquisition of new skills. The latter is the more straightforward and is not dealt with here. The former is much more challenging and demands a willingness on the part of the individuals themselves to explore their own origins, motivating forces and attitudes.

The assertion is that the better individuals understand themselves and understand others' individuality, the more able they will be to effect, understand, manage or accept change and to operate in a team framework. Chapter 8 provides and references a number of techniques to assist such personal development.

COMMUNICATING CHANGE

Clearly the vital link between individuals within and between teams is effective communication.

At its most superficial, communication is a process of data exchange. In a Change Management context, simple exchange of information, that is, the change agent advising of the intended change and receiving comment and reaction, will not suffice. It may achieve awareness or even demand compliance but it will fall far short of the requirement for true commitment to the change and the resultant 'ownership'.

At a deeper level, communication will effect a common under-standing of the intended change and common perspectives over specific issues. Essentially, consensus will be reached. This does not mean that everybody agrees on each and every issue but rather that all those impacted are prepared to 'live with' the proposed change. This definition of consensus may be contrary to conventional wisdom but is crucial to Change Management since any expectation of agreement of all parties is unrealistic in most instances.

Achievement of consensus as so defined will demand that the change agents are able to see and take account of other people's points of view rather than merely defending their own and trying to argue others around to it. Thus the influence exerted to break down resistance involves understanding the needs, concerns and perspec-tives of others.

To develop such influence will effectively demand that the agents of change put themselves into the shoes of those on the receiving end of the change. In so doing, they will appreciate what will satisfy the moti-vating forces of those individuals. In this respect a number of the techniques in the 'Individual Development' chapter (Chapter 8) will be particularly useful. They can be used not only to identify one's own managerial type, driving forces and personality type but to determine the same characteristics in others. This will enable the change agent to comprehend how best to develop a rapport which will lead to credi-bility and to trust.

For example, based upon Quarto's Hilltops **(see pages 112–14)**, you can see how differently individuals might react to the same set of change proposals:

■ those with a 'product' drive will be satisfied by pragmatic and measurable changes which will improve efficiency;

▪ those with a 'people' drive will be satisfied by changes which will improve morale by being in everyone's best interests;

▪ those with a 'process' drive will be satisfied by changes with sound intellectual foundations and which will introduce flexibility into working practices;

▪ those with a 'power' drive will be satisfied by changes which will increase profitability and/or their own personal status;

▪ those with a 'plans' drive will be satisfied by changes which can be logically justified and fit existing operational and procedural frameworks;

▪ those with a 'positioning' drive will be satisfied by changes which will integrate and bond at individual, team and corporate levels;

▪ those with a 'purpose' drive will be satisfied by changes which are innovative and which support and facilitate the achievement of personal and corporate visions.

In summary it is reasonable to suggest that meeting the expectations of each and every individual will be extremely difficult. The purpose of the discussion above is to highlight the importance of endeavouring to anticipate the full consequences of proposed change with a view to identifying which will appeal to the various individuals who form the body of people who will be impacted by the change.

On a positive and final note, it is worth commenting that any well thought through change will contain most of the desirable components recorded above. The issue is simply one of highlighting the right ones to the right people!

Part Two

The Change Management Toolkit

4

Techniques and Models for Establishing the Current Situation

STRUCTURED INTERVIEWS

Purpose

A technique to elicit answers to a series of questions targeted at a number of interviewees in a situation where it is important to ensure consistency of the questions asked of each, eg in an environment in which one interviewee is being compared with another.

What are the principal components of your job ?
How much time do you spend on each component ?
How many people report to you ?
What functions do they perform ?

Method of Operation

1. Define the questions to be asked and commit them to a checklist.

2. If possible, test-run the questions to ensure that the list is comprehensive – this will avoid revisiting interviewees to gather additional information.

3. Validate responses from early 'live' interviews to ensure data collected meets requirements.

4. If required, tabulate the results when all interviews are complete. Given the consistent number and nature of the questions this will be a simple process.

Comments

Structuring interviews is very straightforward but frequently overlooked. Unstructured interviews result in unstructured data which is difficult to analyse and therefore likely to sacrifice credibility.

Structured interviewing is most useful for *establishing the current situation* but may also have value when validating proposals prior to their *planning and implementation*. In both instances, structure provides objectivity in a situation where subjectivity would introduce an undesirable bias. Structured interviews are also valuable during selection interviewing when there are multiple candidates.

Links to Other Techniques or Models

No specific links.

Reference

None.

SPANS OF CONTROL ANALYSIS

Purpose

A technique to establish the ratio of subordinates to managers and the number of hierarchical layers in an organisation.

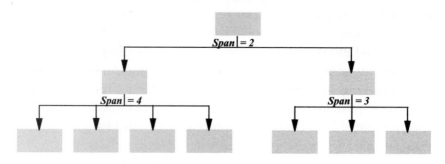

Method of Operation

1. Acquire an accurate structure chart for the division, department or section under investigation.

2. Working from top to bottom, tally under each managerial position the number of direct subordinates. This is the span of control.

3. Tally the numbers of levels between the most senior and most junior (inclusive) positions for the leg of the chart with the greatest number of intermediate positions. This is the number of hierarchical layers.

Comments

In a process re-engineered environment, the accepted wisdom is that:

■   spans of control between six and thirteen are ideal. It is suggested that with a span of less than six, a manager will have too great an opportunity to 'do' rather than to manage;

▪ there should be no more than four hierarchical layers from Chief Executive to the lowest graded member of staff if a high quality of management and flow of communication is to be achieved.

This very simple technique is particularly effective in *establishing the current situation* where a management structure is believed to be becoming top heavy, ie where the opportunity to delayer exists, and in assessing the validity of new management structures prior to their *planning and implementation.*

Links to Other Techniques or Models

No specific links.

Reference

None.

CONCENTRATION DIAGRAMS

Purpose

A technique to facilitate the tracking of the whereabouts of specific 'events'. Typically these events are product defects or problem areas within a process and this technique enables their location and frequency of occurrence to be established.

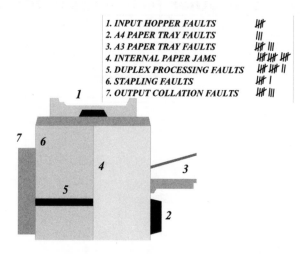

1. INPUT HOPPER FAULTS	JHT
2. A4 PAPER TRAY FAULTS	III
3. A3 PAPER TRAY FAULTS	JHT III
4. INTERNAL PAPER JAMS	JHT JHT JHT
5. DUPLEX PROCESSING FAULTS	JHT JHT II
6. STAPLING FAULTS	JHT I
7. OUTPUT COLLATION FAULTS	JHT III

Method of Operation

1. Identify the 'event' to be tracked.

2. Determine a means of data collection. Examples might be:

   - a plan of the layout of the area in which the 'event' is occurring;

   - an illustration of the product incurring the 'event' (defect);

   - an example of the product itself;

   - a process-map of the process within which the 'event' is occurring;

–   a checklist listing the zones within the overall location in which the 'event' is occurring, eg the shopfloor, warehouse and receiving dock of a supermarket or the motor, electrical connections, handle assembly and clippings box of a lawnmower.

3. Determine who is best placed to collect the 'event' data.

4. Record the 'event' data as appropriate, eg by adding crosses to a layout plan to show location of the 'event', or by five-bar-gate scoring on a checksheet. Data should be recorded until such time as an adequate sample has been obtained.

5. Evaluate results to determine action to resolve the root cause of the 'event'.

Comments

The accuracy of data collection is paramount within the compilation of concentration diagrams and care should be exercised when determining how, and by whom, data is to be collected particularly when large geographical areas are under examination.

Data sample size is also critical and, as a general rule, if in doubt increase the sample size.

Links to Other Techniques and Models

Frequency Diagrams   – page 54

Reference

None.

FREQUENCY DIAGRAMS

Purpose

A technique to determine whether a relationship exists between two variables and, if so, the strength of the influence of one variable upon the other, eg the effect of increases in temperature on the consumption of domestic drinking water.

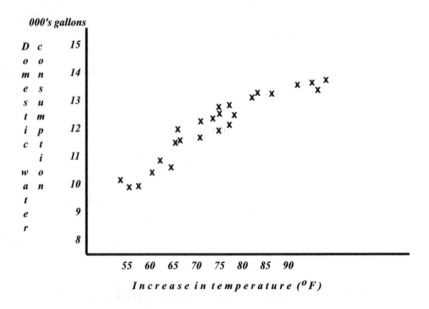

Method of Operation

1. Identify the two variables between which a relationship is believed to exist.

2. Collect sets of data relative to the relationship.

3. Plot the data from each data set on a graph which on the horizontal axis is scaled for the 'cause' variable and on the vertical axis for the 'effect' factor (maximum values applicable to each axis

will be determined by reference to values within the data sets). For repeat data it may be necessary to determine a form of notation, eg a cross at the point of intersection for first occurrence which is circled for second occurrence.

4. Determine whether a relationship exists. This is usually the case if an increase in the 'cause' variable has an obvious proportional or exponential impact on the 'effect' variable.

Comments

Frequency Diagrams are often also referred to as 'Scatter Diagrams'. It is important to be cautious when identifying 'cause' variables. In the event of any suspicion that a wrong conclusion is being drawn, validate the findings with further sample data sets and consider what other variables might result in the 'effect' observed. This consideration of other possible 'cause' variables can effectively be progressed through 'Brainstorming' and 'Cause and Effect Analysis'.

Links to Other Techniques and Models

Reference

None.

CAUSE AND EFFECT ANALYSIS

Purpose

A technique to categorise possible causes of a problem (the 'effect').

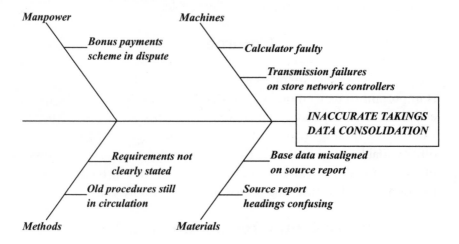

Method of Operation

1. Draw a chart identical to that shown above with the problem (the 'effect') clearly stated on the right hand side.

2. Annotate the chart to indicate the problem categories on the tips of the arrows which face the problem itself. You may select your own categories if you wish but generally those shown, manpower, machines, methods and materials, will encompass the possible causes of a problem.

3. Invite those impacted by the problem to indicate their ideas of possible causes against the appropriate headings to build up a complete picture for detailed analysis.

4. If required, any or all of the identified possible causes may then become the focus of another Cause and Effect Analysis to break the issue down further in order to establish which are the true root causes.

Comments

Perhaps the single greatest merit of this technique is its potential visibility. An appropriately displayed chart, that is, one posted in the vicinity of the problem itself, provides a mechanism by which any party impacted by the problem can suggest possible causes. Such involvement of the overall workforce, rather than an especially selected group, in the problem analysis can promote good team spirit and thus this is also an excellent technique for *teambuilding*.

Cause and Effect diagrams are also known as 'Fishbone' diagrams.

Links to Other Techniques or Models

No specific links.

Reference

None.

PROCESS MAPPING

Purpose

A technique to chart the current activities involved in achieving a particular objective and their interrelationship.

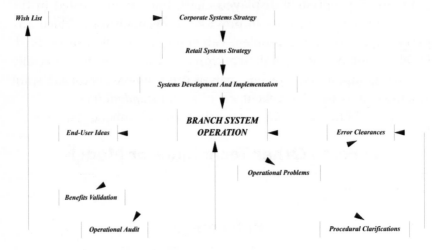

Method of Operation

1. Identify all of the component parts of the current process and commit each to a 'Post-it'.

2. Establish the dependencies of each component to others and move 'Post-its' to define logical sequences of events.

3. Establish component activities or sequences which can parallel other components or sequences and move 'Post-its' to illustrate these parallel relationships.

4. Add lines and arrow connections to connect activities and sequences and illustrate the flow of activity.

5. (optional) For clarity, realign 'Post-its' to place the 'primary' process (the one to which other activities and parallel processes contribute) in a straight line across or down the overall chart.

6. (optional) Add to each component or sequence the name of the party responsible for its completion. This may help to identify inefficiencies resulting from 'hand-offs' between parties.

Comments

This technique is frequently used during Business Process Re-engineering to *establish the current situation*. It could also be used to illustrate a proposed new process during the *planning and implementation* stage of a change situation.

Process mapping is essentially a form of flowcharting and users may wish to increase clarity by using proper flowchart symbols, as shown in Figure 9 below.

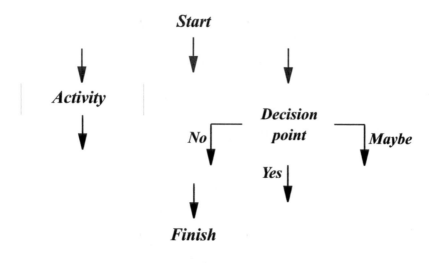

Figure 9

Links to Other Techniques or Models

Critical Path Analysis   – page 63

Reference

None.

PA'S FOUR-BOX MODEL

Purpose

A model to establish a current situation and the reasons for a situation being as it is (stages 1 and 2) prior to determining a better way of achieving the same result (stage 3) and subsequently determining how to put the new methods of working into practice (stage 4).

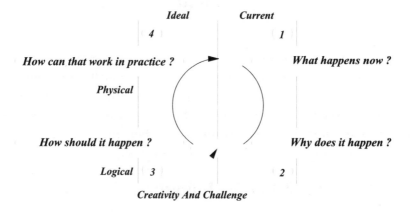

Ideal *Current*

4 *1*

How can that work in practice ? *What happens now ?*

Physical

How should it happen ? *Why does it happen ?*

Logical *3* *2*

Creativity And Challenge

Method of Operation

1. Establish what happens now (the 'current physical' – quadrant 1) by using appropriate techniques for *establishing the current situation*.

2. Question why it happens as it does (the 'current logical' – quadrant 2).

3. Challenge the current practice by considering how the objective(s) of this activity would be best achieved if the methods were being designed from scratch. Use of appropriate techniques for *generating solutions* will enable the redesign of the current

methods in a manner which will eliminate preconceived ideas and facilitate radical thought processes.

4. Determine how it should happen in the future from the options generated (the 'ideal logical' – quadrant 3).

5. Establish how the redesigned process can be put into practice (the 'ideal physical' – quadrant 4) using *planning and implementation* techniques.

Comments

This simple model provides a powerful thinking structure by means of which change requirements can be determined. It is frequently used for radical Business Process Re-engineering but is equally applicable to change on a smaller scale. The model spans the entire change process from *establishing the current situation* through *generating solutions* to *planning and implementation*. For maximum benefit, it is critical that the right techniques are chosen to progress each stage (see below).

Links to Other Techniques or Models

Stage 1:	Structured Interviews	– page 48
	Brainstorming	– page 68
Stage 2:	Brainstorming	– page 68
Stage 3:	Brainstorming	– page 68
Stage 4:	Consensus Reaching	– page 72
Stage 5:	Brainstorming	– page 68

Reference

The Four-Box Model is included by kind permission of PA Consulting Group, 123 Buckingham Palace Road, London.

CRITICAL PATH ANALYSIS

Purpose

A technique to chart the current activities involved in achieving a particular objective, their interrelationship, the timescales for completion of each component activity or activity sequence and, consequently, the 'critical path' activities (those that must be completed and in a sequence which will determine the duration of the full process).

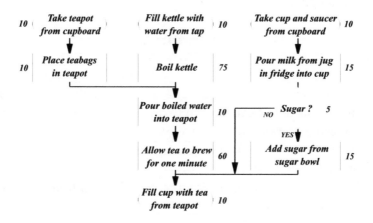

Method of Operation

1. Identify all of the component parts of the current process and commit each to a 'Post-it'.

2. Establish the dependencies of each component to others and move 'Post-its' to define logical sequences of events.

3. Establish component activities or sequences which can parallel other components or sequences and move 'Post-its' to illustrate these parallel relationships.

4. Add lines and arrow connections to connect activities and illustrate the flow of activity.

5. Determine the sequence of activities leading to the ultimate process objective which has the longest duration and place this 'critical path' process in a straight line across or down the chart.

6. Establish the 'slack' which exists within the contributory processes and indicate against each. This will enable you to identify where such processes might start later, finish earlier or contain 'slack' between component activities without adverse effect on the 'critical path'.

Comments

Critical Path Analysis (CPA) is a well-established, well-respected, sophisticated analysis technique. The description above is very basic but many books have been written to describe CPA in detail. There are also increasing numbers of software packages available for CPA which will add still greater sophistication, eg resource analysis and stylish presentation.

CPA can be used to *establish the current situation* and during *planning and implementation*.

Links to Other Techniques or Models

Process Mapping   – page 58
Block Schedule   – page 82

Reference

None.

5

Techniques and Models for Generating Solutions

COST OF QUALITY ANALYSIS

Purpose

A model to identify the relationship between those activities typically employed to ensure the achievement of a high quality result (product

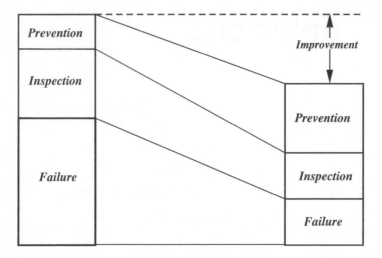

or process) and specifically to illustrate the value of preventative measures as opposed to post-completion or post-production inspection and/or the reworking of failures (defective products).

Method of Operation

1. Identify the component parts of a production or other process.

2. Determine whether each component represents 'basic work',

'preventative measures', 'inspection' or response to 'failure'.

3. Determine how new or enhanced preventative measures might be introduced to reduce the need for inspection.

4. Identify root causes of failures to determine how they might be eliminated through the introduction of new or enhanced preventative measures or production and process methods.

Comments

Application of this model is common in a Total Quality environment where the elimination of waste (failure) is key to project by project improvement. It is a very straightforward approach to the analysis of work components although some conclusions will depend on the perspective of those completing it. For example, conducting a survey of customer requirements might be considered prevention by a Retail Store Manager but represent basic work to the Market Research department.

Links to Other Techniques or Models

Stage 1:   Process Mapping   – page 58
Stage 2:   Consensus Reaching   – page 72
Stage 3:   Brainstorming   – page 68
Stage 4:   Concentration Diagrams   – page 52
           Frequency Diagrams   – page 54
           Cause and Effect Analysis   – page 56

Reference

None.

BRAINSTORMING

Purpose

A technique for generating large numbers of ideas around a common theme from a group of people in a very short period of time.

> *IMPROVING SYSTEMS STRATEGY*
> *Involve the customers (branches)*
> *Agree cost/benefit in advance*
> *Establish strategy think tanks*
> *Set a minimum rate of return on investment*
> *Full dummy configuration for testing*
> *Involve end-users in system testing*
> *Benchmark against competitors*
> *Use only one hardware platform*
> *Bring back cash registers*
> *Don't over-engineer systems*
> *Build-in support tools*
> *Visit trade fairs to view new technologies*

Method of Operation

1. Gather an appropriate group together. Typically, this will comprise those with a vested interest in the problem or issue under debate, that is, those involved with, or impacted by it.

2. Advise the group of the problem or issue and check that all participants fully understand.

3. If appropriate break the issue down into manageable topics, eg 'the complexity of developing IT solutions for retail stores' might

split into 'how to generate the right original specification', 'how to design appropriate systems', 'how to test a system effectively' and 'how to implement a system cost effectively'. State the sub-issue which the group are to tackle first and note it at the top of a flipchart page.

4. Invite the members of the group to call out their suggestions to resolve the problem or issue. Record every idea, as stated, on the flipchart so that the developing list is visible to the group. Encourage succinct statements.

5. Do not allow discussion or criticism and aim for quantity not quality.

6. Permit laughter at wacky ideas – they often have tremendous potential – but quash ridicule of group members when they present ideas which may seem outrageous.

Comments

Brainstorming is a powerful, versatile and simple technique for generating ideas but demands disciplined facilitation by the group leader (who should not participate in the ideas generation process itself). It can be applied to almost any problem or change issue and can be used at any stage in the change process. Maximum benefit will be derived by linking a basic brainstorming session to other techniques as suggested below.

Links to Other Techniques or Models

Affinity Diagrams   – page 70
Consensus Reaching   – page 72

Reference

None.

AFFINITY DIAGRAMS

Purpose

A technique to provide an initial structure to an already-generated set of ideas.

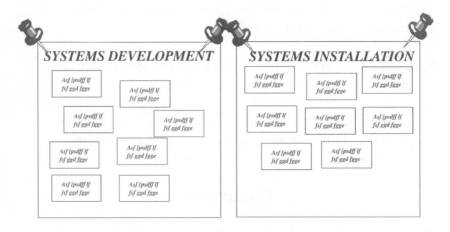

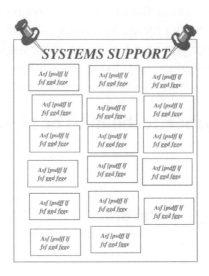

Method of Operation

1. Commit a set of random ideas to 'Post-its' – one idea per 'Post-it'.

2. Stick all of the 'Post-its' onto a wall or similar.

3. Move 'Post-its' in order to group together on pieces of flipchart paper those which have similar and/or connecting themes.

4. Determine titles which capture the theme of each group of 'Post-its' and write these titles on the top of the individual flipchart pages above the group of 'Post-its' to which they relate.

5. If appropriate, move the flipcharts themselves into a sequence which links one to another.

Comments

The set of random ideas may have been generated by means of a brainstorm or by another group or individual process. Establishing affinity between ideas and groups of ideas may similarly be a group or individual process which can be applied to ideas relating to almost any problem or change issue at any stage in the change process.

Links to Other Techniques or Models

Brainstorming – page 68

Reference

None.

CONSENSUS REACHING

Purpose

A technique to determine the best or most popular options or ideas in circumstances where many possibilities, which may be randomly presented, exist.

IMPROVING SYSTEMS STRATEGY
1. Involve the customers (branches)
2. Agree cost/benefit in advance
3. Establish strategy think tanks
4. Set a minimum rate of return on investment
5. Full dummy configuration for testing
6. Involve end-users in system testing
7. Benchmark against competitors
8. Use only one hardware platform
9. Bring back cash registers
10. Don't over-engineer systems

1.   6 points
10. 3 points
9.   1 point

7.   7 points
10. 3 points

Method of Operation

1. Present all of the possible options or ideas which have been identified on a single page to the group of people responsible for their original formulation.

2. Number each option or idea.

3. Award each member of the group a set number of voting points and invite all participants to cast their votes in whatever manner they wish, ie one may choose to award all of his points to his favourite option or idea, another may spread his votes across a number of appealing options or ideas. Each participant should record his voting privately. Alternatively ask each group member to rank, say, his ten favourite options or ideas, awarding maximum points to his favourite, one less point to second favourite, and so on.

4. Capture all scores on a single flipchart and establish a ranking.

5. If required, through repeating the process for, say, the top dozen options or ideas, or through discussion of those most favoured, elicit the single most favoured option or idea.

Comments

The original set of random options or ideas may have been generated by means of a brainstorm or by another group or individual process. Voting in isolation to establish the best options or ideas is fraught with danger – individuals must be expected to justify their own voting once a group score has been established and discussion must ensue. Nevertheless, this simple technique can be applied to almost any set of options or ideas at any stage in the change process to promote a healthy discussion and assist the achievement of consensus.

Links to Other Techniques or Models

Brainstorming – page 68

Reference

None.

6

Techniques and Models for Planning and Implementation

FORCEFIELD ANALYSIS

Purpose

A technique to identify those forces which assist or obstruct the implementation of change.

User Involvement In Systems Development

Driving Forces	Restraining Forces
Users' motivation and interest	Budgetary constraints
Ownership requirement	Systems knowledge requirement
Users' right of veto	Store staffing pressures
Proven quality benefits	Understanding of overall strategy
Radical thinking	Impact on development timescales
Knowledge of store needs	Integration into development team
"Jury service" possibility	

Method of Operation

1. Describe the planned change in a simple sentence at the top of a flip chart.

2. List the driving forces which support the planned change on the left hand side of the chart.

3. List the restraining forces which may obstruct the planned change on the right hand side of the chart.

4. Determine which of the restraining forces pose the greatest threat to change and highlight them for specific action.

5. Determine which of the driving forces represent the best levers for implementing change and highlight them for specific action.

Comments

Identification of the forces favouring or threatening change can be beneficial in determining whether to progress the planned change and, if so, how best to overcome the identified restraining forces and maximise use of the driving forces. It should be noted that breaking down the barriers to change will generally be more effective than promoting the favourable forces.

Links to Other Techniques or Models

Stages 2 & 3: Brainstorming   – page 68
Stages 4 & 5: Consensus Reaching   – page 72

Reference

None.

THE LEAVITT/BAHRAMI DIAMOND

Purpose

A model to emphasise the importance of balancing change in business structure with technical issues, people issues and associated control mechanisms to ensure change is effected appropriately.

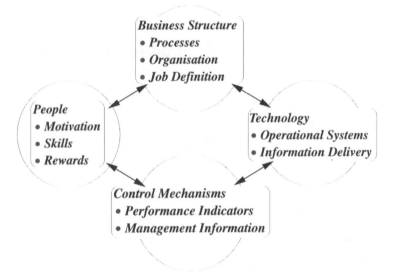

Method of Operation

Examine the change scenario under consideration to:

▨ identify how new processes are supported by technology both for their operation and for their ability to deliver information;

▨ identify how organisational changes and consequent redefinition of job roles are matched by people management techniques which equip personnel with appropriate skills and motivate and reward those individuals;

▌ determine whether the people management changes are appropriately underpinned by control mechanisms in the form of performance indicators;

▌ ensure that information delivery within the new processes is appropriately consolidated through Management Information Systems and human effort which is performance-measured.

Comments

This model provides a simple but effective checklist for Change Management which draws together four critical components which must all be considered in order to invoke successful change.

It is worth noting that the 'People' category is the most often over-looked in large and hierarchical organisations probably because it generally tends to be the last to be considered in a change management setting and is the most subjective. In a situation in which the workforce has not been extensively involved in initiating or implementing change it is likely to be the most difficult to address because of people's natural resistance to change.

McKinsey's 7 Ss may be regarded as a more specific version of this model but the simplicity of the Leavitt/Bahrami Diamond will be preferred by many.

Links to Other Techniques or Models

McKinsey's 7 Ss   – page 80

Reference

Leavitt, H J and Bahrami, H, *Managerial Psychology*. The University of Chicago Press Ltd, London
© 1958, 1964, 1972, 1988 by The University of Chicago. All rights reserved. Published 1988. Fifth edition 1988.

McKINSEY'S 7 Ss*

Purpose

A model to assess the readiness of an organisation for change through validation of the alignment of the corporate strategies with six other critical internal factors.

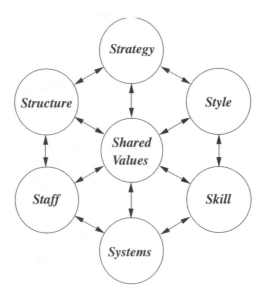

Method of Operation

In relation to the defined strategic intent, assess whether:

▓   Corporate *values* are widely *shared* with, and held by, members of the workforce and whether individuals recognise and accept their part in achieving the corporate strategies and/or change.

▓   An appropriate managerial *structure* has been established or can be successfully implemented to support the proposed change.

* Copyright © 1982 by Thomas J Peters and Robert H Waterman, Jr
Reprinted by permission of HarperCollins, Publishers, Inc

- Managerial *style* will 'champion' the proposed change. If the change demands devolution of power in an autocratic organisational culture, will managers contemplate a change which invokes an associated loss of personal authority?

- The proposed change demands a high level of commitment and, if so, whether such commitment can reasonably be expected from the *staff*. This is likely to depend on the value placed on staff by the company and attitudes to staff displayed by Management.

- The appropriate *skills* exist within the workforce or, if not, whether plans have been made to acquire such skills which will not be resisted by individuals or, perhaps, union activity.

- *Systems* have been accurately defined to support the proposed change. In this context, systems comprise both IT solutions and other techniques for proceduralisation, automation, and collation and dissemination of information.

Comments

This model must be regarded as a checklist for Change Management which identifies seven core components, none of which must be overlooked. The Leavitt/Bahrami Diamond is a simpler model but many will prefer the more comprehensive headings assigned by this model which are easily memorised because of the linking Ss.

Links to Other Techniques or Models

The Leavitt/Bahrami Diamond — page 78

Reference

'MCKINSEY'S 7S FRAMEWORK' from *In Search Of Excellence: Lessons From America's Best-Run Companies*, Thomas J Peters and Robert H Waterman, Jr (1982), HarperCollins

BLOCK SCHEDULE

Purpose

A technique to aid the planning process (and particularly, the planning of activities between major milestones) and to illustrate graphically an implementation plan.

Project Nemesis Implementation Plan

	1996												
	April				May				June				July
	8	15	22	29	6	13	20	27	3	10	17	24	1
PHASE ONE													
Staff Briefings	■												
Management Workshop		■											
PHASE TWO													
Internal Announcement				■									
Press Conference													
PHASE THREE													
Staff counselling					■	■							
Office moves							■	■	■				
Management review												■	

Method of Operation

On squared paper or using an appropriate PC spreadsheet software package (the latter offering considerably greater flexibility):

■ create a matrix of dates (day, week, month or other intervals as appropriate) on the horizontal axis and activity slots on the vertical axis;

■ identify known milestones (fixed or targeted critical dates) for activities and a list of the intermediate, but as yet unplanned, activities between milestones;

- insert the list of activities in chronological sequence into the activity slots running down the left hand side of the matrix;

- for milestones, block-shade the cell at which the description and its fixed or targeted date intersect;

- for all remaining intermediate activities determine an appropriate schedule which ensures the achievement of milestones and block-shade accordingly.

Comments

Considerable value can be added to a basic Block Schedule through the addition of:

- a title indicating the purpose of the schedule;

- different shades or colours to highlight particular activities, eg those on the 'critical path';

- notation instead of shade or colour within the body of the schedule which can be related to a key at the base of the schedule, if required;

- a 'Who' column adjacent to the activities which specifies the party or parties responsible;

- a marker along the horizontal axis to indicate current date;

- a date of schedule production and, if relevant, a version number;

- subheadings within the activity list on the vertical axis for logical activity subgroups.

Links to Other Techniques or Models

Critical Path Analysis — page 63

Reference

None.

7

Techniques and Models for Teambuilding

RICH PICTURES

Purpose

A technique designed to introduce team members to one another in a relaxed and interesting manner thereby building understanding of team member's individual backgrounds and maximising the potential for teamwork.

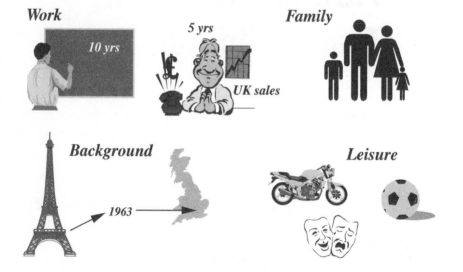

Method of Operation

1. Invite each member of the group to draw, on a sheet of flipchart paper, pictures depicting:

    –   his working life to date

    –   his family environment

    –   his personal background

    –   his interests outside of work

    –   one thing which members of the team are unlikely to know about him, eg an amusing or unusual life event, an unusual hobby or an unusual claim to fame.

2.   Invite each member of the team, in turn, to present and explain their 'rich picture'.

Comments

The principal virtues of this approach to team introductions are firstly, its slightly frivolous nature which serves well to break the ice and, secondly, its visual nature which will make a more vivid and memorable impression. Additionally, it is likely that some of the individuals' personal values will emerge in pictorial form and be readily understood by other team members.

The exercise would be applicable both to newly-formed teams and to existing teams whose members, for whatever reason, are relatively unacquainted. It is important, in either instance, to advise members of the group that they need only reveal about themselves what they feel able to reveal – none must feel embarrassed by obligation.

Links to Other Techniques and Models

Getting To Know One Another   – page 88
Sharing Visions, Values, Beliefs and Dreams   – page 91

Reference

None.

GETTING TO KNOW ONE ANOTHER

Purpose

A technique to generate improved teamwork by establishing a better understanding of the backgrounds of the individual members.

Method of Operation

1. Devise a simple proforma (see Figure 10) to establish some basic facts about the individuals within the group. Typically, this will be similar to the biodata one might collect in a job application form or during a job interview.

2. In a team setting, distribute sufficient copies to team members to enable each to complete one in respect of every other individual present.

3. On completion and starting with yourself, as group facilitator, invite the group to suggest their answers. Provide correct answers to each question and award a point to each individual who has the right answer. Continue until all questions have been considered.

4. Ask for a volunteer to continue the process within the group and repeat until all group members have been dealt with.

5. Invite group members to tally their scores for each individual and compare scores against the maximum possible for the proforma.

'DON'T I KNOW YOU FROM SOMEWHERE?'

Name	:
Age	:
Career History	:
Marital Status	:
Names/Ages of Dependants	:
Town of Residence	:
Country/Town of Origin	:
Leisure Pursuits	:
Religious Persuasion	:

....

Partner's Name	:
Partner's Occupation	:
Partner's Employer's Name	:
Partner's Country/Town of Origin	:
Partner's Leisure Pursuits	:

'PERHAPS I DON'T REALLY KNOW YOU AT ALL!!!'

Figure 10

Comments

This is a simple but powerful exercise which must, for maximum effect, be introduced in a light-hearted manner and within a team framework. It is vital to respect each individual's privacy and allow actual answers to questions to be passed over if this is threatened (in which case, simply amend the maximum possible score for the individual concerned). Do not worry unduly about the proforma design – it is surprising just how little people do know about each other and the exercise will therefore hold good. The exercise can be used with both new and existing teams to create or reinforce team spirit.

Links to Other Techniques or Models

Rich Pictures   – page 86
Sharing Vision, Values, Beliefs and Dreams   – page 91

Reference

None.

SHARING VISIONS, VALUES, BELIEFS AND DREAMS

Purpose

A technique to foster teamwork through open and honest sharing of personal motivating forces in order to improve mutual understanding of work attitudes.

Method of Operation

In a team environment, ask each individual to spend time independently determining the following with a view to sharing them with the group later in the session:

1. **His personal vision**: this may include the individual's personal aspirations in respect of career, personal relationships and family, his vision for the company, department or group in which he works, his vision of the outcome of a particular event, or project, etc.

2. **His personal values**: this will include those factors which determine the way the individual typically acts in work and/or domestic circumstances. Examples might be high value placed on absolute accuracy, quality of presentation, the importance of consensus or respect for others' views and opinions, etc. Typically, these are values the individual will not be prepared to compromise.

3. **His beliefs**: these will most probably be the underlying factors which shape the individual's attitudes. For example, a deep religious conviction, a concern for the environment or belief in the rights of animals might respectively shape the individual's attitudes to the use of bad language, production processes and blood sports.

4. **His dream**: this may be the individual's perceived ultimate destiny. Alternatively, it may be one or more life ambitions and may have short-, medium- or long-term status.

Comments

It is recommended that the four items suggested above are considered and presented in the sequence given since there is a progressively deeper fathoming of the individual's motivations in each stage. Sharing of one's dreams is very powerful in terms of enabling others to understand one's core motivation but sharing of any of the above must be a voluntary act.

Links to Other Techniques or Models

Rich Pictures   – page 86
Getting To Know One Another   – page 88
Fritz's Creative Visualisation   – page 121

Reference

None.

THE POWER OF METAPHOR

Purpose

A technique by which a simple but important message can be effectively conveyed.

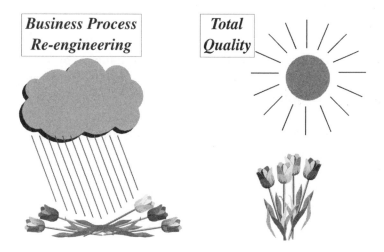

Method of Operation

1. Determine the content of the message to be conveyed.

2. Consider the make-up of the target audience in order to determine the sort of visual images to which they will best relate.

3. Create an appropriate picture in your mind and then commit it to paper, eg a flipchart page.

4. Display the picture to the target audience and offer a brief description of the manner in which it encapsulates your message.

Comments

This technique exploits the philosophy that 'a picture paints a thousand words' and the well-established fact that visual messages are more effective than aural ones (a message combining the two being still more powerful).

In the example above, Business Process Re-engineering is portrayed as a dark cloud raining down and flattening the flowers on the ground; the cloud representing top-down management, the flowers being the workforce and the rain being the top-down imposition of process re-engineering. Total Quality, by comparison, is portrayed as glorious sunshine warming the workforce and encouraging them to grow and to reach ever higher and, in so doing, to contribute positively to the surrounding environment.

Links to Other Techniques or Models

Rich Pictures   – page 86
Sharing Visions, Values, Beliefs And Dreams   – page 91

Reference

None.

OD&D'S INTERPERSONAL INFLUENCE INVENTORY

Purpose

A technique to enable an individual to assess how he influences others.

High	*Openly Aggressive Behaviour*	*Assertive Behaviour*
	I boldly insist that my rights and needs prevail	*I clearly express that we both have rights and needs*
Openness in Communication	*Concealed Aggressive Behaviour*	*Passive Behaviour*
	I subtly make sure that my rights and needs prevail	*Others' rights and needs take precedence over mine*
Low	*Consideration for Others*	**High**

This technique results in an individual being categorised as having a behaviour which falls within one of the four categories shown above based upon his openness in communication and his consideration for others.

Some basic characteristics for each category are detailed in Figure 11.

Openly Aggressive Behaviour

Openly aggressive behaviour results when an individual employs a high degree of candour, yet gives little consideration for the thoughts and feelings of the other party. Aggressive behaviour may be defined as domineering, pushy, self-centred and self-enhancing. A person who is openly aggressive in the extreme may be abusive, threatening and authoritarian. His non-verbal behaviour may take the form of glaring, finger pointing or angry movements toward the other party.

Concealed Aggressive Behaviour

Concealed aggressive behaviour results when a person is neither candid as to his motives nor considerate of the other person's rights. A concealed aggressive finds subtle ways to convey his reactions and feelings. For example, a manager may exclude an unsatisfactory subordinate from critical meetings as a way of suggesting that he look for another job. Neither the openly aggressive nor the concealed aggressive gives others much consideration. The difference between the two is a matter of directness. One is up front and unconcerned with others; the other is subversive and unconcerned with others.

Passive Behaviour

Passive behaviour is inhibited, self-denying and conflict avoidant. The passive individual ignores his own needs and feelings in an attempt to satisfy the needs and feelings of others. As a result, he experiences feelings of low self-esteem, frustration and sometimes withdrawal. Anger and other feelings are turned inward. Other people are accorded more rights than he accords himself.

Assertive Behaviour

The assertive person is both open and respectful of the rights of others. He is self-revealing, self-respecting, yet able to communicate his thoughts and feelings in ways that do not violate the rights of others. Burley-Allen defines assertiveness as 'an approach to interacting with others based on an active and initiating rather than reacting mode of behaviour; a caring position, emphasising the positive nature of self and others; self-expression through which one stands up for his basic rights without denying the rights of others and without experiencing undue anxiety or guilt; a non-judgmental attitude that diminishes the use of labels, stereotypes and prejudices and communicating wants, dislikes and feelings in a clear, direct manner without threatening and attacking'.[1]

Figure 11

Method of Operation

Utilisation of this technique entails:

1. Completion of a copy of OD&D's *Interpersonal Influence Inventory* by indicating against each statement given whether it is completely uncharacteristic, quite uncharacteristic, somewhat characteristic, quite characteristic or completely characteristic of you. Respectively, these score 0, 1, 2, 3 and 4 points.

2. Totalling your scores on the grid provided which splits the 40 statements across four categories of behaviour – assertive, passive, concealed aggressive and openly aggressive.

[1] *Managing Assertively* Burley-Allen (1983)

3. Plotting your scores on the graph provided to determine how they compare with averages calculated from a sample of other managers.

4. Referencing the explanatory notes which provide further background on norms and describe the four styles thus assisting their interpretation.

5. Identifying a small number of colleagues (superiors, peers and subordinates) and asking them to complete the analysis about you.

6. Totalling and plotting the scores indicating carefully your own scores and those of others and comparing their perception of you with your self-perception.

Comments

Since this technique measures interpersonal relationships and specifically assertion, aggression and passivity, real value is added to this exercise through the completion of Stages 5 and 6 which will highlight the manner in which you are perceived. Further value will be added if the whole exercise is conducted within a team framework in which every member completes the analysis for himself and for the other members of the team with an open and honest discussion of results ensuing.

Links to Other Techniques and Models

Senn-Delaney's Behaviour Styles – page 99

Reference

Interpersonal Influence Inventory © 1990 by Dr Rollin Glaser
With permission of Organization Design and Development, Inc
King of Prussia, Pennsylvania

In the UK, OD&D's *Interpersonal Influence Inventory* can be obtained from Management Learning Resources Ltd, PO Box 28, Carmarthen, Dyfed

SENN-DELANEY'S BEHAVIOUR STYLES*

Purpose

A technique to enable an individual to establish his behavioural style based on his own perception and that of close colleagues.

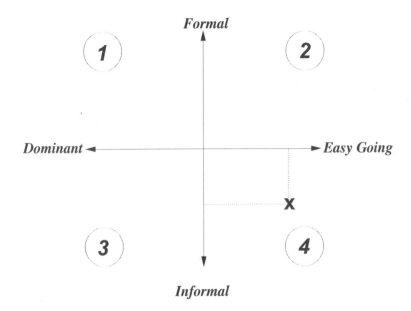

Method of Operation

1. In a team environment, each team member should draw the intersecting axes illustrated above and label them as shown.

2. Each should then plot a point along the horizontal axis to indicate the extent to which they tend, in a normal working environment,

to be dominant or easy going and on the vertical axis a point to indicate the extent to which they tend to be informal or formal.

3.   Once complete, lines should be drawn from the two plotted points, at right angles to the axes, into the quadrant in which they will intersect. The individual should initial the point of intersection.

4.   Each individual's chart should then be passed among the team who will repeat stages 2 and 3 in respect of every other member of the group.

5.   Each completed chart should then be returned to their originators for him to consider the explanatory notes in Figure 12 which name and describe the behavioural styles represented by each of the four quadrants and any variance between self-perception and the perception of others.

Strengths	Challenges
1. Controlling Style (formal, dominant)	
▪ great at achieving results – results-focused ▪ fast decision-makers ▪ disciplined ▪ self-motivated, hard workers ▪ goal-oriented ▪ persistent, focused, not easily distracted from goal ▪ will confront problems easily – don't avoid ▪ strong need to succeed	▪ can be insensitive to hurting other people's feelings ▪ can ignore others' needs in order to achieve end result ▪ likes to do things themselves rather than educate others ▪ can be impatient ▪ not good listeners ▪ likes things 'my way' ▪ others feel tense and pressured around them
2. Analysing Style (formal, easy-going)	
▪ systematic, orderly and organised ▪ plan things in advance ▪ rarely make big mistakes ▪ logical, rational, pragmatic, realistic, rarely get overly emotional	▪ find it hard to make decisions ▪ can be too perfectionistic – get upset if things aren't perfect ▪ can get upset if something gets in way of plan ▪ don't like to take risks

<ul><li>conscientious</li><li>thorough and comprehensive, cover all bases</li><li>good problem-solvers</li><li>don't like doing a lot at once – what they do, they do right and thoroughly</li></ul>	<ul><li>hard to know where they stand because they don't show feelings</li><li>procrastinate – put things off</li><li>inhibited – not spontaneous</li></ul>

3. Promoting Style (informal, dominant)	
<ul><li>come up with new ideas – creative</li><li>get others excited about new ideas</li><li>high energy, enthusiastic, fun to be around</li><li>persuasive</li><li>sociable, outgoing, friendly</li><li>spontaneous</li><li>enjoy fast-moving challenge</li><li>like to be active, doing many different things</li></ul>	<ul><li>start more things than finish</li><li>don't plan ahead – do things at last minute</li><li>disorganised – let things fall through the cracks, poor follow-through</li><li>can be seen as a 'con' because are so excitable and tend to exaggerate stories to get others excited</li><li>can be too impulsive – act before thinking</li><li>get bored easily</li><li>unrealistic in expectations</li></ul>

4. Supporting Style (informal, easy going)	
<ul><li>sensitive, tuned-in to feelings of others, considerate of others</li><li>good team players</li><li>close relationships are high priority</li><li>patient and empathetic</li><li>dependable</li><li>good listeners</li><li>easy to talk to, calming to be around, looked to by others for support</li><li>in conflict, able to give up needing their way</li></ul>	<ul><li>difficult for them to give feedback if it is something other person may not like</li><li>hate conflict – would rather avoid or give in than confront</li><li>hide feelings, and resentment builds because don't like to confront</li><li>gauge own self-worth by reaction of others</li><li>can't say no – get stuck doing things they don't want to</li><li>too accepting and permissive</li></ul>

Figure 12

Comments

It is not essential for group members to initial their entries on others' charts. However, since behaviour in a group environment is being measured, openness and honesty are paramount and value will be added to the exercise if frank discussion of results ensues.

Links to Other Techniques and Models

OD&D's Interpersonal Influence Inventory — page 95

Reference

Included with the kind permission of the Senn-Delaney Leadership Consulting Group Inc, of Long Beach, CA.

PA'S GAINING COMMITMENT ('TWO ARROW DIAGRAM')

Purpose

A model and associated technique which serves to illustrate, on a sliding scale, the difference between awareness of proposed change and dedication to that change and, by so doing, to help gain commitment to change from those who will be impacted.

Communication	*I have been told*	*Awareness*
	I understand what I've been told	*Understanding*
Involvement	*I am contributing facts and ideas*	*Contribution*
	I am helping to shape ideas	*Engagement*
Commitment	*I like the look of that : let's do it*	*Support*
	I realise this is a very hard path; let's still do it	*Obligation*
	Not only is this a hard path but it will affect me fundamentally; let's do it anyway	*Dedication*

Method of Operation

1. Display the leftmost column of the chart as shown above to those impacted by the proposed change and explain that your intention is to examine with the group the difference between communication of change and commitment to change, the middle ground being some limited involvement in change formulation.

2. Reveal the rightmost column of the chart and explain that awareness and understanding are facets of having received communication about proposed change, contribution and

engagement are facets of involvement while support, obligation and, ultimately, dedication represent real commitment to change.

3. Reveal the middle column and allow the group to digest how each quote exemplifies the states previously identified.

4. In respect of the proposed change, ask each group member to determine their current position.

Comments

Successful change demands commitment from the parties impacted as well as those engaged in change formulation and implementation. The greater the number of individuals who feel and demonstrate commitment, the higher the probability of success.

It is suggested that the earlier an individual is made aware of the demands of change on him the more likely it is that he will be able to make the transition from low level awareness to real dedication. It is therefore appropriate to introduce this model at the earliest possible opportunity and to return to it repeatedly in order to reinforce its crucial message.

Links to Other Techniques or Models

No specific links.

Reference

The Two Arrow Diagram is included by kind permission of:
PA Consulting Group, 123 Buckingham Palace Road, London and the model's originator, Mel Eastburn, a former Director of PA Consulting Group

OWEN'S OPEN SPACE TECHNOLOGY

Purpose

A technique which permits the discussion of issues of particular concern to individuals within an open, non-threatening framework of meetings.

Whoever comes is the right people.
Whatever happens is the only thing that could have.
Whenever it starts is the right time.
When it's over, it's over.

Method of Operation

To employ this technique:

1. Organise and publicise a 'themed' but agenda-less meeting which anybody who wishes to may attend in order to participate in the discussion of issues yet to be specifically defined but relevant to the theme.

2. Open the meeting by inviting all those who have issues they wish to discuss to note their issue on a sheet of A4 paper and to announce them to the assembled group. Advise attendees that anyone suggesting a topic must be prepared to facilitate the initial group discussion.

3. Ask each volunteer to add his name (as facilitator) and then display all topic notices along the length of a wall.

4. Invite the entire group to 'sign-up' for every discussion group in which they wish to participate by adding their names to the appropriate notices.

5. Based upon the total number of discussion group topics nominated and the time available, create and display a timetable matrix identifying venues and start and finish times for sessions.

6. Explain that sessions will run in parallel in order to ensure all topics can be accommodated but that this should not prevent individuals attending every group in which they have an interest since there will be no obligation to stay for the complete duration of a session (although if they are facilitating they must ensure that another individual takes up this role).

7. Advise that there is no obligation to attend any group if none is of interest in a particular timeslot or indeed throughout the session.

8. Start the first group of sub-meetings.

Comments

Although a simple technique, the preparatory organisation and initial facilitation is critical to its success. The Appendix to Owen's book *Riding The Tiger* contains a substantial number of hints and tips for this introductory process which are commended to first-time users.

Links to Other Techniques and Models

No specific links.

Reference

Owen, H (1991) *Riding The Tiger*, Abbott Publishing, Potomac, Maryland (USA)

8

Techniques and Models for Individual Development

LESSEM'S SPECTRAL MANAGEMENT TYPE INVENTORY

Purpose

A technique to enable an individual to determine his preferred (dominant) managerial 'type(s)' and associated style(s).

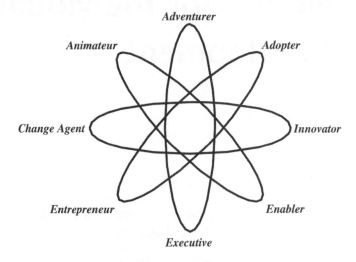

The technique results in an individual being categorised as one of the eight managerial 'types' identified above for each of which some basic characteristics are detailed in Figure 13. As a mnemonic and for ease of reference each 'type' is related to a 'spectral' colour as follows:

Adventurer	– red	**Executive**	– blue
Animateur	– orange	**Enabler**	– indigo
Change Agent	– yellow	**Innovator**	– violet
Entrepreneur	– green	**Adopter**	– grey

Lessem's Adventurer	Lessem's Executive
energetic	authoritative
work hard/play hard	structure and strategy
reactive	deliberative
doer	organiser
spirit of adventure	spirit of leadership
Lessem's Animateur	**Lessem's Enabler**
charming	magnetic
shared values	harnesses potential
responsive	harmonic
animator	reflector
spirit of community	spirit of development
Lessem's Change Agent	**Lessem's Innovator**
enthusiast	charismatic
flexible	vision
experimental	inspired
networker	creative
spirit of freedom	spirit of creativity
Lessem's Entrepreneur	**Lessem's Adopter**
dynamic	humble
enterprise	service
energised	contemplative
initiator	reflector
spirit of enterprise	spirit of quality

Figure 13

Method of Operation

Utilisation of this technique entails:

1. Completion of an eight-question questionnaire in which you rank the eight answers given for each by awarding eight points to the answer most typical of you, seven points to the next most typical and so on with one point only awarded to the answer least typical of you.

2. Transferring the scores to a scoring grid and totalling scores by each of the 'spectral colours'.

3. Establishing their ranked order: 1 for the highest score (dominant style/'type'), 2 for the second highest score and so on, and thus determining your 'spectral colour', managerial style and managerial 'type'.

4. Referencing Figure 13 above for an overview of the characteristics of these 'types' and Lessem's book *Total Quality Learning* Chapters 6, 7 and 10 for much more comprehensive descriptions of all but the 'Adopter'.

Comments

When referencing *Total Quality Learning*, examine the descriptions of your dominant type and second and third ranked types as a minimum – this is particularly important if the differentials between the scores are small.

It is suggested that your time will, in fact, be well spent reading the descriptions of all of the 'types' since this will effectively permit you to establish, in managerial terms, those characteristics which are not typical of you as well as those things which are.

Once you have validated your own analysis in this way, seek the qualitative validation of a trusted friend.

Links to Other Techniques and Models

Quarto's Hilltops   – page 112 and Appendix 1

Reference

Lessem, R (1991) *Total Quality Learning* Basil Blackwell Ltd, Oxford

Lessem's Spectral Management Type Inventory can be obtained from R Lessem PhD, University of Buckingham, Hunter Street, Buckingham.

QUARTO'S HILLTOPS

Purpose

A technique to enable an individual to discover his driving forces and to understand that others may have different drives and may view the world and other people from a different 'hilltop'.

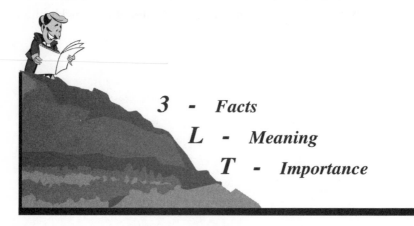

3 - *Facts*

L - *Meaning*

T - *Importance*

Method of Operation

Quarto's paperback *First Find Your Hilltop* defines seven categories of driving force: 'product', 'people', 'process', 'power', 'plans', 'positioning' and 'purpose'. Figure 14 details basic characteristics of each and to a greater or lesser extent you will relate to some or all of them.

Each driving force is discussed in substantial detail in Quarto's book together with a technique to determine their importance to you. This technique is known as '3LT' (the '3 Level Technique'). To use '3LT' to determine your driving forces, for example, in respect of your career, you would:

1. Pose the question 'what do you do ?' This establishes the basic 'facts'.

2. Consider 'what you get out of doing it ?' This establishes the 'meaning'.

Quarto's Product Drive	Quarto's Plans Drive
▪ action	▪ order
▪ physical activity	▪ structure
▪ pragmatism	▪ logic
▪ common sense	▪ rationality
	▪ organisation
Quarto's People Drive	**Quarto's Positioning Drive**
▪ friendship	▪ intuition
▪ caring	▪ meaning
▪ a sense of belonging	▪ sensitivity
▪ acceptance	▪ integration
▪ loyalty	▪ balance
Quarto's Process Drive	**Quarto's Purpose Drive**
▪ change	▪ vision
▪ new experience	▪ mission
▪ variety	▪ imagination
▪ intellectual stimulation	▪ creativity
Quarto's Power Drive	
▪ energy	
▪ commitment	
▪ challenge	
▪ success	
▪ recognition	

Figure 14

3. Question 'why is the "meaning" (your basic motivation) important to you?' This establishes the 'importance'.

Having considered various questions relating to each drive in turn and thus assessed its 'importance' on a scale of 1 to 10, it is possible to complete a histogram of the results and to establish their relative importance to you.

Comments

Having discussed the seven drives and enabled you to establish their relative importance, Quarto's paperback continues by commending validation of your results by a third party. Practical advice is then offered in respect of developing specific drives and using one's new-found self-knowledge to make career and other life changes.

Links to Other Techniques and Models

Lessem's Spectral Management Type Inventory	– page 108 and Appendix 1
Schein's Career Anchors	– page 123

Reference

Calvert, R; Durkin, B; Grandi, E and Martin, K (1990) *First Find Your Hilltop* Hutchinson Business Books Ltd, London

REWRITING THE SCRIPTS

Purpose

A technique through which an individual may (re-)examine the impact of others on his life to date particularly those who have, or could have, exerted influence.

Method of Operation

1. Create a simple list of those whom you believe have had a significant impact on your life to date at a personal level. Typically, this will include parents and other relations, teachers, employers and friends.

2. Take each individual in turn and determine whether you consider their influence to have been positive or negative. Ask yourself whether you blame the individual for some unsatisfactory aspect of your present situation.

3. For those whose influence you continue to consider as unsatisfactory, ask yourself whether their influence was deliberately malicious or simply a failure to meet your expectations.

4. In the event that you identify malicious intent, remind yourself that 'what's done is done'.

5. Where individuals have failed to meet your expectations, ask yourself whether your expectations were too high and whether, in reality, the individuals in question did everything they could have done in the circumstances. Where this is the case, 'rewrite the script' in your mind to reflect this new understanding. Where you remain unconvinced that this is the case, consider whether you might give the individual the benefit of the doubt in order for you to obviate the blame and to be able to get on with your life.

Comments

Many individuals go through life with misperceptions or unhelpful perceptions of the influence others have had upon life's course. This can result in continually blaming one's current circumstances on past events and failing to face up to reality and to take control of one's own destiny. This exercise has the potential to 'unlock' such an unfortunate situation.

Links to Other Techniques and Models

Peale's Positive Thinking – page 117

Reference

None.

PEALE'S POSITIVE THINKING

Purpose

A technique by which an individual may correct an inappropriate attitude or 'mind-set' in respect of a particular issue or situation.

Method of Operation

Usage of the positive thinking technique assumes that you have first identified an inappropriateness of your attitude to your current or perceived future circumstances. For example this might apply if, as a result of events, you have come to doubt your own ability and have, perhaps, allowed your negative thinking to develop into what is sometimes referred to as 'awfulising'. This being the case:

1. *'For the next 24 hours, deliberately speak hopefully about everything, about your job, about your health, about your future. Go out of your way to talk optimistically about everything.'** This can be achieved by

---

* italicised text is from Peale's *The Power of Positive Thinking* – see Reference

repeating aloud or in your mind, positive affirmations relating to your ability or potential.

2. *'After speaking hopefully for 24 hours, continue the practice for one week, then you can be permitted to be "realistic" for a day or two. You will discover that what you meant by "realistic" a week ago was actually pessimistic, but what you know mean by "realistic" is something entirely different; it is the dawning of the positive outlook.'*

3. *'Feed your mind even as you feed your body, and to make your mind healthy you must feed it nourishing, wholesome thoughts.'* In essence, treat yourself to a positive thinking 'diet' on an ongoing basis.

Comments

Positive thinking as described above can be used in two ways:

▨ to revitalise/rebuild self-esteem when circumstances have caused you to cast doubt on your actual abilities;

▨ to convince yourself that you have the potential to meet future challenges when, in fact, you are uncertain of your potential but wish to rise to an opportunity.

Arguably, the latter is a form of personal 'brainwashing' and as such, should be treated with caution lest you should end up 'biting off more than you can chew'. The former is a very valid and effective means of re-establishing your feelings of self-worth.

Links to Other Techniques and Models

Re-writing the Scripts – page 115

Reference

Peale, N V (1953) *The Power Of Positive Thinking* Cedar, London

THE KUBLER-ROSS GRIEF CYCLE

Purpose

A model to illustrate the typical cycle of reactions an individual will experience in a situation in which he loses something held dear. The model was originally created to illustrate reaction to bereavement but is equally applicable to other forms of loss, eg job loss or unwanted change or loss of a partner through divorce or separation.

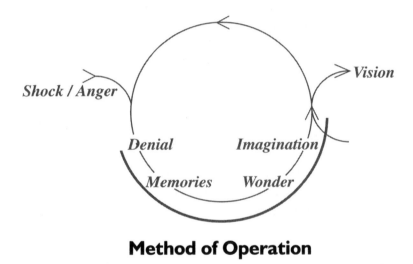

Method of Operation

The identified stages of the cycle are:

1. **Shock** followed by **anger** directed at the perceived cause of the loss. The latter may not be rational and may be self-focused, focused upon the cause of the event or even on the victim of the event, eg in the event of bereavement, on the person who has died.

2. **Denial** will almost certainly follow as you consciously or subconsciously insist that the event has not, indeed could not have, happened.

3. Then as you begin to accept, **memories** will occupy your mind. Within this stage there may be regrets for things which might have been said and, perhaps, for things left unsaid.

4. Accompanying the start of recovery, **wondering** about the future is probable as you question how things will be different following the loss.

5. This should lead to **imagination** as you actively seek to shape possible futures. From this may emerge the **vision** which you will actively pursue and which will break the cycle. This is the critical point since failure to 'lock on' to a positive future may result in the perpetuation of the cycle as you fail to find real future purpose.

Comments

This powerful model enables individuals to recognise the grief cycle in their own lives or those of others faced by serious loss. It is appropriate to urge caution – none of the stages must be hurried. The affected party must have time both to grieve and to envision a positive future. The most beneficial stance close relations, friends and colleagues can adopt is one of 'being there' as a shoulder to cry on – a willing listener, and to offer non-directive encouragement. Any more prescriptive intervention is best left to trained counsellors whose involvement, in the majority of cases, does not need to be invoked.

Links to Other Techniques and Models

Fritz's Creative Visualisation (for the Vision stage)   – page 121

Reference

Kubler-Ross, E (1973) *On Death and Dying*, Routledge, London

FRITZ'S CREATIVE VISUALISATION

Purpose

A technique which employs the natural 'tension' between current reality and future vision to facilitate the achievement of that vision.

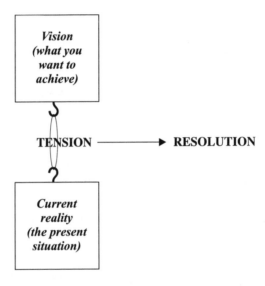

Method of Operation

This technique entails:

1. Envisioning the desired situation in respect of a particular issue, eg formulating a vision of your ideal career or job situation.

2. Objectively describing current reality in respect of the issue.

3. Objectively, and without regard to perceived feasibility, describing what you want to achieve (your vision) and then validating the accuracy of the description and the desirability of achieving this vision by simply asking yourself whether, if the desired state were attainable now, you would choose it.

4. Formally, and consciously, choosing the desired state in a simple statement to yourself such as 'I choose to be a self-employed electrical contractor'. This affirmation will reinforce your ultimate objective in your mind.

5. Continuing normal daily life but witnessing how your recognition of your desired state compels you to conduct yourself and your affairs in ways which work towards your 'Utopia'.

Comments

The stages above describe Fritz's 'pivotal' technique which generates a 'structural tension' between the current and desired states which seeks resolution in the form of achievement of the latter. Within this simple but powerful process, it is essential that both the current reality and the desired state are articulated with the maximum possible accuracy and that, in order to maximise the 'structural tension', the latter genuinely represents the ultimate vision insofar as it can be envisioned at the present time. Techniques such as the use of meditation may assist the envisioning process.

This technique can be employed both for personal and business objectives.

Links to Other Techniques and Models

Schein's Career Anchors   – page 123

Reference

Fritz, R (1984) *The Path of Least Resistance* Ballantine Books, London

SCHEIN'S CAREER ANCHORS

Purpose

An exercise to enable an individual to determine career-related values or 'anchors', that is, those facets of a career which are held most dear and which must be present in a future career opportunity.

Method of Operation

Schein's book *Career Anchors* defines eight such 'anchors'. In order to determine reliably those which are important to you, Schein promotes an interview process with validation through a 'Career Orientations Inventory'. This entails:

1. Selecting a partner by whom you are willing to be interviewed and who you feel able to interview in respect of past career and life decisions.

2. Completing the 41-question 'Career Orientations Inventory' contained within Schein's book and advising your partner to do likewise.

3. Using the interview questions provided, conducting the mutual interviewing process.

4. Matching the interview career themes against the eight categories of career anchor and ranking them in order of importance. Your partner should do likewise.

5. Individually scoring the 'Career Orientations Inventory' using the marking scheme provided and use the resultant ranking to validate the 'manual' ranking which resulted from the interview process.

6. Investigating discrepancies with your interview partner through reference to his interview notes and through examination of individual questions within the Inventory which led to that ranking. One or other ranking should be amended as appropriate.

7. Swapping roles and repeating the process in respect of your partner's discrepancies.

8. Discussing with your partner the implications of the results for your current and future careers.

Comments

It is important to identify an interview partner with whom you will feel at ease and who will treat your discussions confidentially. It is also essential to focus on reality rather than a desired state, and on the present and the future rather than the past. This is without doubt a valuable exercise, the validity of which is strengthened by the cross-checking against the Inventory score.

Links to Other Techniques and Models

No specific links.

Reference

Schein, EH (1993) *Career Anchors* Pfeiffer and Co, San Diego, California (USA)

Appendix I
Lessem's Spectrum and Quarto's Hilltops – A Comparison

Lessem's Adventurer	Quarto's Product Drive
energetic	action
work hard/play hard	physical activity
reactive	pragmatism
doer	common sense
spirit of adventure	
Lessem's Animateur	**Quarto's People Drive**
charming	friendship
shared values	caring
responsive	a sense of belonging
animator	acceptance
spirit of community	loyalty
Lessem's Change Agent	**Quarto's Process Drive**
enthusiast	change
flexible	new experience
experimental	variety
networker	intellectual stimulation
spirit of freedom	

Lessem's Entrepreneur	Quarto's Power Drive
dynamic	energy
enterprise	commitment
energised	challenge
initiator	success
spirit of enterprise	recognition
Lessem's Executive	**Quarto's Plans Drive**
authoritative	order
structure and strategy	structure
deliberative	logic
organiser	rationality
spirit of leadership	organisation
Lessem's Enabler	**Quarto's Positioning Drive**
magnetic	intuition
harnesses potential	meaning
harmonic	sensitivity
reflector	integration
spirit of development	balance
Lessem's Innovator	**Quarto's Purpose Drive**
charismatic	vision
vision	mission
inspired	imagination
creative	creativity
spirit of creativity	

Appendix 2
CD ROM User Guide

The notes that follow detail the content of the CD ROM and provide guidance on the use of the CD ROM files.

FILE TYPES

All files are provided in Microsoft Office '97 format. Individual documents are of one of the following file types:

▌ Microsoft Office '97 files:

- Word (.doc extension) word-processing files;

- PowerPoint (.ppt extension) graphics files;

- Excel (.xls extension) spreadsheet files.

CD ROM STRUCTURE

The CD ROM directory structure mirrors the chapters and sub-sections of the *Change Management* book. The sub-directory for each Change Management model contains a number of documents of the types described below.

Document Types

▪ **'How to' documents** contain the full text of the relevant section of the *Change Management* book, describing the operation of each Change Management model.

▪ **'Image' documents** contain the graphics used in the book to depict the Change Management model described within a section.

▪ **'Worked example' documents** contain the graphics used in the book to depict a particular deployment of the Change Management model described within a section.

▪ **'Blank proforma' documents.** These files contain templates to facilitate the use of a particular model, and are derived from the 'image' or 'worked example' documents.

▪ **'Symbols' documents.** These files contain graphics – the symbols required when using particular Change Management models.

▪ **'Style descriptors' documents.** These tables contain the full descriptive text from a relevant section of the book for those Change Management models which, when used, define individual styles, characteristics or attributes.

DOCUMENT MODIFICATION

Subject to any third-party copyright restrictions noted, the author grants permission for the content of any of the CD ROM files to be modified as the user sees fit to meet his specific need.

DIRECTORY STRUCTURE

D: *(where D: is the drive name of the User's CD ROM)*
1. Change, Corporate Culture and Change Management
   – Context of Change Model   (.ppt)
   – Change Management Principles   (.doc)

2. Types of Change
   – The TQ Temple   (.ppt)
   – Supplier–Customer model   (.ppt)
   – The BPR Temple   (.ppt)
   – Cross-functional Process Model   (.ppt)
3. Teambuilding, Individual Development, Change, Communication
   – Commitment to Change Model   (.ppt)
4. Establishing the Current Situation
   – Structured Interviews
       How to   (.doc)
       Image   (.ppt)
   – Spans Of Control Analysis
       How to   (.doc)
       Worked example   (.ppt)
   – Concentration Diagrams
       How to   (.doc)
       Worked example   (.ppt)
   – Frequency Diagrams
       How to   (.doc)
       Worked example   (.ppt)
   – Cause and Effect Analysis
       How to   (.doc)
       Blank proforma   (.ppt)
       Worked example   (.ppt)
   – Process Mapping
       How to   (.doc)
       Symbols   (.ppt)
       Worked example   (.ppt)
   – PA's Four-Box Model
       How to   (.doc)
       Image   (.ppt)
   – Critical Path Analysis
       How to   (.doc)
       Symbols   (.ppt)
       Worked example   (.ppt)
5. Generating Solutions
   – Cost of Quality Analysis
       How to   (.doc)
       Image   (.ppt)

- OD&D's Interpersonal Influence Inventory
  How to   (.doc)
  Image   (.ppt)
  Style descriptors   (.doc)
- Senn-Delaney's Behaviour Styles
  How to   (.doc)
  Image   (.ppt)
  Blank proforma   (.ppt)
  Style descriptors   (.doc)
- PA's Gaining Commitment
  How to   (.doc)
  Image   (.ppt)
- Owen's Open Space Technology
  How to   (.doc)
  Image   (.ppt)

8. Individual Development
   - Lessem's Spectral Management Type Inventory
     How to   (.doc)
     Image   (.ppt)
     Style descriptors   (.doc)
   - Quarto's Hilltops
     How to   (.doc)
     Image   (.ppt)
     Style descriptors   (.doc)
   - Re-writing the Scripts
     How to   (.doc)
     Image   (.ppt)
   - Peale's Positive Thinking
     How to   (.doc)
     Worked example   (.ppt)
   - The Kubler-Ross Grief Cycle
     How to   (.doc)
     Image   (.ppt)
   - Fritz's Creative Visualisation
     How to   (.doc)
     Image   (.ppt)
   - Schein's Career Anchors
     How to   (.doc)
     Image   (.ppt)

Bibliography

Burley-Allen (1983) *Managing Assertively,* John Wiley & Sons Inc., New York (USA)

Calvert, R; Durkin, B; Grandi, E and Martin, K (1990) *First Find Your Hilltop,* Hutchinson Business Books Ltd, London

Fritz, R (1984) *The Path Of Least Resistance,* Ballantine Books, London

Glaser, Dr Rollen (1990) *Interpersonal Influence Inventory*

Hammer, M and Champy, J (1993) *Re-engineering the Corporation,* Nicholas Brealey Publishing, London

Hutchins, D (1992) *Achieve Total Quality,* Director Books, Hemel Hempstead

Kubler Ross, E (1973) *On Death And Dying,* Routledge, London

Leavitt, H J and Bahrami, H (1988) *Managerial Psychology,* University Of Chicago Press (USA)

Lessem, R (1991) *Total Quality Learning,* Basil Blackwell Ltd, Oxford

Owen, H (1991) *Riding The Tiger,* Abbott Publishing, Potomac, Maryland (USA)

Peale, N V (1953) *The Power Of Positive Thinking,* Cedar, London

Peters, T J and Waterman (Jr), R H (1982) *In Search Of Excellence: Lessons From America's best-run companies,* Harper Collins, New York (USA)

Schein, E H (1993) *Career Anchors,* Pfeiffer and Co, San Diego, California (USA)

Index

NB: numbers in italics indicate charts, figures or tables